A Life After Loss

A Personal Story of Grief and Hope

Annalysa Alonzo

CLAY BRIDGES
PRESS

A Life After Loss

A Personal Story of Grief and Hope

Copyright © 2021 by Annalysa Alonzo

Published by Clay Bridges in Houston, TX
www.ClayBridgesPress.com

Scripture quotations marked MSG are taken from THE MESSAGE, copyright © 1993, 2002, 2018 by Eugene H. Peterson. Used by permission of NavPress, represented by Tyndale House Publishers. All rights reserved.

Scripture quotations marked (NLT) are taken from the Holy Bible, New Living Translation, copyright ©1996, 2004, 2015 by Tyndale House Foundation. Used by permission of Tyndale House Publishers, Carol Stream, Illinois 60188. All rights reserved.

Scripture quotations marked ESV are from The ESV® Bible (The Holy Bible, English Standard Version®), copyright © 2001 by Crossway, a publishing ministry of Good News Publishers. Used by permission. All rights reserved.

Scripture quotations marked NLT are taken from the Holy Bible, New Living Translation, copyright © 1996, 2004, 2015 by Tyndale House Foundation. Used by permission of Tyndale House Publishers, Inc., Carol Stream, Illinois 60188. All rights reserved.

Scripture quotations marked (NIV) are taken from the Holy Bible, New International Version®, NIV®. Copyright © 1973, 1978, 1984, 2011 by Biblica, Inc.™ Used by permission of Zondervan. All rights reserved worldwide. www.zondervan.com The "NIV" and "New International Version" are trademarks registered in the United States Patent and Trademark Office by Biblica, Inc.™

ISBN: 978-1-953300-73-7
eISBN: 978-1-953300-72-0

TABLE OF CONTENTS

INTRODUCTION

*O*nce upon a time, there was a young girl who dreamt of things far beyond what anyone thought was possible. She was a quiet girl with no concept of what her life purpose could possibly be. When her dreams finally became a reality, however, everything changed. The life she once dreamt of fell away in a split second, and the trials and tribulations she faced were impossible feats never conquered by anyone in her life before.

Her life course changed; she was suddenly in a new place, alone, left to discover for herself what is left when you lose what you thought your future would hold. Out of this shadowed place in her life, she found a new purpose, led by a new light. She rediscovered what she already knew, found strength in her faith, and walked with Jesus.

This is no fairy tale. The girl in this story isn't a book character or a metaphor for the potential of loss. The girl in this story is me, and my story does not have a traditional happily ever after.

After years of contemplating how to share my life experiences with others, and years of doubt and fear about sharing things that are very personal and painful, there comes a time when you just have to take the leap. Questions always arise when baring your story to the world, running through my head (Are they going to like me? Is what I'm doing enough? Is what I have done enough?), but at this point in my life, those questions no longer matter.

Life is too short to worry about what other people think of you, and if this story can help even one person who might also be going through the type of loss and process that I went through, then it needs to be shared. This story isn't to glorify my doings. All the glory belongs to God. I hope that this story helps you. I pray that you see the light that is Jesus and that He guides you to the other side.

But even if you don't believe, I hope that this book encourages you to share your story, in your own voice, no matter who you are or where you are in life. You never know the effect your words can have, and you never know who your story can save.

Part 1:

A Change of Plans

"We plan the way we want to live, but only God makes us able to live it" (Proverbs 16:9 MSG).

I'm the type of person who makes plans just for the sake of making plans, but let's be honest; God's plans are far greater than ours.

How do you put something like this into words? The unfathomable, the unspeakable, the unimaginable. How do you write into existence an experience that no one should have to endure? How do you share something so misunderstood, and often times unrelatable, with the rest of the world?

Honestly, I don't know. But here goes nothing.

Something unheard of happened on the morning of September 1st, 2016. Here's what I knew: I was going to be a mother. I knew I was going to be responsible for raising and loving a beautiful human being, and I knew my life was going to change forever.

It was around Christmas of 2015 when I found out I was pregnant. I had absolutely no idea or feeling, no natural instinct that just told me I was going to have a baby. My boyfriend, let's call him AJ, knew though. Immediately.

I know it may seem strange that I, with my faith, did not wait until marriage to have sex or start a family. Even if it doesn't seem strange in today's world, I feel it is important to acknowledge that I was not married when I became pregnant and that the journey that led to me sharing this story would not exist if I had waited. This is a testimony to how God changed my life, and mistakes are a part of that. I am only human, and I know that I have an amazing God who died for our sins. AJ and I both longed for that close relationship with our creator, but we prioritized ourselves in the relationship and not God. That was our shortcoming.

We were together for 11 months, almost a year, and we knew that we were madly in love with each other. Time, however, was our worst enemy. Eight months into our relationship I was accepted into the college of my dreams, the Fashion Institute of Design and Merchandising. I always wanted to travel the world and attend fashion shows. I wanted to be the person that styled the models or help set up fancy events and shows. It was my dream, my goal, and I was on my way. The problem? Distance.

The institute was in Los Angeles, a two-hour distance from AJ. We did our best and made it work, but the weekend after Christmas, our world was meant to change. He came down to visit on the 26th and I was so excited to show him where my dreams would soon come true. We went to the mall I worked at and took in all the beautiful Christmas decorations, we got delicious Chinese food and Sprinkle cupcakes, and made such a beautiful memory of our time together. It was a day neither of us would forget.

When we got back to my house, he immediately asked if I would take a pregnancy test because he had a feeling. I laughed it off at first, saying there was no way I could be pregnant. I had no symptoms, everything was normal. But he insisted, so we went back out and found the nearest drug store. In my disbelief, I bought five tests, because I just needed to be sure.

I remember being in the bathroom waiting impatiently as the results came up on the first test. I don't even think I remember all of them, it was such a blur, but five tests later I had five positives.

Everything happened so fast after that. I was on my knees in tears, denial taking over me. Grief isn't just something felt for lost loved ones, but also for the loss of a potential future, and I felt it then. The guilt for being upset also hit me. People fight to become pregnant so often that it felt unappreciative to feel this way. It was a blessing, but it certainly did not feel that way that first night I took the tests.

Part 1: A Change of Plans

AJ had always wanted a family of his own, but I was only twenty. I wasn't ready to be a mother. I begged time to slow down, to go back. I believe now that was the bargaining phase.

And just like that, my time in Los Angeles at my dream school ended. One of the biggest accomplishments of my life became a short memory. While I know many mothers who still go to school and reach their career aspirations, I needed to be around family at this time in my life, so I moved back home.

Home Sweet Home

Have you ever been so excited to leave a place and start a new journey somewhere different just to find yourself returning to where you started just a few months later? That's exactly what the return home felt like.

I'm from a small, remote desert town in California. There isn't much there except desert (like cacti and tumbleweeds), and hot weather. I had always dreamed of leaving that town and venturing out into the world, so of course, the moment I was able to move to Los Angeles I was ecstatic!

Now, having to return home, all I could think about was how disappointed everyone would be.

I decided to first tell my grandparents about me being pregnant.

My grandparents have been married and in love for over 40 years. They are the craziest but most loving people in the world, and I absolutely adore them. My grandfather came from Mexico to the United States when he was a young boy. He met a beautiful blonde-haired, blue-eyed girl in high school, they fell in love, and the rest is history. Despite the many challenges and differences they had over the years, their love always brought them back together.

I pray to have the type of love that they have one day.

I was so excited to share with them that they were going to be great grandparents. I am the oldest grandchild (and the most adored in my opinion) so everything I experienced was a first. I most certainly still expected disappointment, but once the words "I'm pregnant" came out of my mouth their reactions surprised me. The shock was there of course, but they were so excited to extend their love to my growing baby, their new great grandbaby.

My parents were another case entirely. They had me when they were still teenagers in high school. My mother was turning fifteen and my father was just one year older. Although I was still older than them at this point, I did not feel any better about breaking the news.

My dad was still in the military at the time, so I had to tell him over the phone. How do you tell your dad something like this over the damn phone? Please excuse my language, but God knows my heart and he also knows who my grandmother is; she always said it was good for the soul. Back to the conversation, the phone was not the ideal way to tell my father the news, but it was all I had. He was very emotional and disappointed of course because he knew what I had planned for myself. My father encouraged me to stick it out and finish school, but I knew in my heart I needed to be home. I was still his little girl to him, and although he had my beautiful baby sister as well, I would always be daddy's little girl.

Going back and forth from two different households wasn't easy for me as a child, and I would not want that for my future family. My mother meeting my stepdad was life-changing in many aspects. I gained more siblings, I gained another parent, and I gained a household that was full of many trials and tribulations, but also full of much love. When my father met my step-mom, it was hard to wrap my head around the idea of now having four parents. I didn't make life easy for her, but I was eternally grateful for all she had done taking on someone else's child as their own. I may not always have shown much appreciation to my stepparents, I love them more than they'll ever know, but they stepped up in ways that have helped shaped who I am today.

Now it was time to tell my mother. My sweet mother, thankfully I got to tell her in person. She had actually just given birth to my miracle of a baby sister that November, so you could imagine all the different emotions she was feeling at once. She cried and I cried, and we cried together. She knew how hard I had worked to reach my goals and get out of that small desert town in California and was sad that I now had to turn back. I'll never forget her words: *"Well, it's time to grow up. Get ready."*

I don't think ready was even within eyesight at that point.

I never imagined having a child, and I especially never imagined having one at the age of twenty-one. My friends always told me that I would be traveling the world, going to fashion shows, and would be a strong independent woman. I was expected to have a fancy loft and drive a nice car, and after years of planning and hearing those expectations I really believed in that version of my future. But everyone was wrong; I was going to be a mother. That was my destiny.

As the denial and disappointment began to evaporate from my heart, I knew I had to come to terms with the fact that God intended other things for my life, and they did not involve being in Los Angeles.

Tough Talks

Why me? Why did you change everything when I finally got everything that I wanted? What is the purpose of this new plan? How do I go on? There were infinite questions of doubt. There were so many questions that I knew I probably wasn't going to get an answer to. I had to be okay with not being able to fully comprehend God's plan for me, at least not all at once. I think we try so hard to understand what we weren't meant to understand. If we knew everything that God had planned for our lives, would we be capable to actually live it? What does it mean to really live? We are meant to live a life for God, a life that is less of us and more of him.

You may ask God, *"So what now? What is my purpose if you've changed my plans? Do I still have a purpose?"* I used to think I didn't serve a purpose on this earth anymore. I mean my parents didn't plan for me. I thought I might have been viewed as just an accident. At least that was where my mind was at. I once heard in a sermon that our purpose is not so much about doing, but more so about who we are becoming. We are human-*beings*, not human-do-ings. I'm sure I could've done marvelous things if I stayed in Los Angeles. But maybe God didn't like who I would've become, or maybe I wouldn't have.

We aren't meant to know all the answers, but we can most certainly be confident in the one who does. Don't be afraid to ask God hard questions. I know what it is like to question God or be afraid to ask him those difficult questions. He wants us to be honest and not hide anything. He knows our hearts and what we long for, but sometimes what we long for may not be good for us. So, what is the point of sharing what you want with God, or telling him how you feel?

Well, God is a great listener; he hears everything you have to say, and he wants to help you. Maybe God saw more potential in my life that I could not imagine at the time. Sometimes it isn't about what God can do for us, but what we can do for him. It's not about who we can be and become by ourselves, but who we can be and become with him. When plans don't go your way, when life isn't going your way, place your life and your plans before God and trust that he will not lead you astray.

> "So here's what I want you to do, God helping you: Take your everyday, ordinary life—your sleeping, eating, going-to-work, and walking-around life—and place it before God as an offering. Embracing what God does for you is the best thing you can do for him. Don't become so well-adjusted to your culture that you fit into it without even thinking. Instead, fix your attention on God. You'll be changed from the inside out. Readily recognize what he wants from you, and quickly respond to it. Unlike the culture around you, always dragging you down to its level of immaturity, God brings the best out of you, develops well-formed maturity in you." (Romans 12:1-2 MSG).

God's Plan

Before I knew it, spring had arrived. After we had both told our families that we were expecting, I announced it publicly on social media platforms. Immediately after, I contemplated deleting the post because I was afraid of what people would think of me. What would my friends say? I was at a point in my life where I was trying to please everyone around me, but I knew this was not something I could hide. It was the cutest announcement though; my cousin wrote "Baby Guinn Arriving September" on a chalkboard and we had placed an ultrasound picture next to it.

Only 6 more months to go.

I was nowhere near ready. I think I've stated that I was not ready about ten times now. Is anyone ever really ready to be a parent? Maybe some are. I know there are plenty of women who just know they want to be mothers, and some men who just know they want to be fathers. I was not one of them, and I was not ready mentally, spiritually, or even physically.

Physically, pregnancy was taking a lot out of me. I had terrible morning sickness that lasted all day. I would vomit anywhere at any time, so going out was never fun. The pregnancy journey was not easy. God blessed the mothers who never had morning sickness! When my body finally began adapting to the beautiful new life forming inside me, I decided to try to get it together again. I transferred to an online university and continued to pursue my education. I also got a desk job as a customer service representative, because I knew having a child was not cheap. It came in handy, not only financially, but also because my feet were so swollen, like bigfoot. I couldn't even fit my foot into a chancla! I also gained about 60 pounds and I felt the weight everywhere.

For those of you who have never met me, I am 4'11.5", maybe 5 feet on a good day. Unless you saw me waddling, you probably wouldn't have noticed I was pregnant if you were behind me. Carrying around all of the extra weight took a huge toll on my body, but every moment was worth it. Feeling the kicks and the baby moving was an overall amazing experience.

When it came time to find out the sex of the baby, I do have some regrets. I would have had more family members there for the reveal; I did not give myself or others any preparation time for any of this but having an extra support system would've been amazing. It was just AJ and I at the time, with a 3D ultrasound. When I saw my baby's face, I did not care what the sex was going to be, but part of me was always team girl. When they started typing "It's a...girl!" I was happier than I could have ever possibly imagined. After talking with each other and a few of our family members we decided to give her a name: Aria Monet Guinn.

I cannot even explain the level of excitement and love I felt when I knew we would have a baby girl. I knew we would have such a great bond, just like my own mother and I had. She is literally my best friend, and even though we disagree on some things or bump heads like in any other mother/daughter relationship, I looked forward to experiencing it all with my own daughter. Getting to experience pregnancy for myself made me really appreciate true motherly love.

While the joy was there, so were the questions. This was still a huge change for me, as I mentioned, on a physical, mental, and spiritual level. I would always ask, "God, why did you change my plans?" This was not in the books for me. I am not ready to be a mom. Why are there stretch marks on my body? Why can't I go back to how things were? Why can't I have my old life back? So many questions crossed my mind all of the time. I still questioned God and what he was doing, not understanding what the future would look like now. There was nothing I could do at this point except trust that whatever plan God was unfolding in my life now, whether I liked it or not.

In my mind, this situation was like a tug-of-war. I could keep trying to pull back and forth with God, trying to make him see how things were better on my side, or I could surrender and let him be in control, and trust in his side. This was a fight I knew I couldn't win. We try so hard to show God how things would be if our plans were to fall accordingly rather than just simply abiding by his. His plans are far greater than ours, whether we want to believe it or not. We may not understand it in the moment, or the next day, week, or even month, but I truly believe he does reveal his truth. The catch, however, is that it is on his time, not ours.

"...Yet I want your will to be done, not mine" (Luke 22:42 NLT).

Almost There

Three more months to go. It was time to plan a baby shower. It was time to shop for diapers and a crib instead of shoes and a matching handbag. It was time to dedicate these next few months solely to this beautiful baby girl growing inside me. It was time to put my selfish needs aside, or better yet away for good. Aria was already so loved by everyone, and we had not even met her yet. My mom was super stoked to plan a baby shower for me, and I am eternally grateful for not just her help, but for the help of my future in-laws as well. Yep, that's right, future in-laws—I'll explain later.

The baby shower was stunning. The decorations were pretty and pink, but most importantly I was surrounded by loved ones. It was a beautiful day, but also a difficult one because it was all starting to feel surreal. Have you ever daydreamed of how your life would be? In this moment of being showered with love, I was also showered in tears. Not bad tears, but good ones. I dreamt of how she would look like in the gifts people had bought her. I'd dress her in a beautiful silk dress and put a pretty bow on her head. I dreamt of how our families would love on her and spoil her. I dreamt of my future as a mother. My new dreams were going to be a reality. Or so I had thought.

Part 1: A Change of Plans

So much change had happened in my life in a matter of months. Has there been a sudden change in your life? It doesn't matter how big or small the change is because it is still a change. We cannot go through these changes alone. I certainly thought I was handling life okay on my own, but now I see that's not how it should be done.

I was terrified that AJ's parents weren't going to like me. I'm such a people pleaser, I just want people to like me. But if I don't fully know who I am, how can I show that to others? I eventually came to the realization that you can't make everyone like you, and that's okay. The only approval I need is God's, not anyone else. Okay, maybe my parents and family but even at that God's approval is still above all.

You can experience real change within yourself when trying to please people. You try so hard to become this idea of a person that you think people want you to be. It's actually quite exhausting. You literally have to put more work into acting a certain way than to just simply be yourself. For example, if they think I'm shy maybe I should speak up more. But if I speak up more, maybe they'll think I'm too loud, or that I am too much, so I should just be quiet.

If they don't like you for YOU, let them take a seat or admire you from a distance. Let the real ones take a stand and appreciate who you are. God was not liked by everyone. Do you think he is liked by everyone now? Unfortunately, no. But that doesn't stop him from doing what he is called to do or be, and it shouldn't stop you either.

Let me rewind way back really quick before I left my little hometown to be a big-time city girl living in Los Angeles. After I graduated from community college, AJ had given me a gift. It wasn't flowers or even a bracelet, but a promise ring! Honestly, I received something like this in high school, but that was short-lived, and a story for a different time. I truly believe we meet people for a reason or just for a season, either way, we learn something new. The meaning behind this beautiful silver ring was a bit bittersweet.

AJ has a big loving family and has told me about his longing for children and marriage while we were dating. I was honest and told him I wasn't certain about kids just yet because of course I wanted to finish school. This also goes back to what my friends had instilled inside my mind of me being single and successful.

Gosh, that sounds so lonely. What is it to have all the riches in the world, and no one to share it with? It's lonely and I didn't want to do it alone. Eventually, we went out on a date and the rest was history. We started going out in January, he actually asked me out after our first date, or maybe I persuaded him to ask me. Either way, I knew I was in love. Four months later, I graduated from community college. I thought, he must really love me if he is giving me a promise ring, right? Does that mean he really does see a future with me too? Despite all the arguments we had, like all other couples, he still wanted to be with me. I thought it was beautiful that he longed for these things, especially at our age because that's very rare to find. When you find something so precious and rare, don't take it for granted.

Know Your Worth

"When you know you are of worth—not asking it but knowing it— you walk into a room with a particular power".

—*Maya Angelou*

I ask myself a lot of questions, which I'm sure you have already discovered by now. I can be indecisive, unsure, and second-guess many things. However, I also want to make sure I have somewhat of an answer ready if need be. If you stay ready, you don't have to get ready, right? So back to the ring. He made me a promise that one day we would get married, and I said yes. He knew I was going to move away to another city and yet he still wanted to be committed to me. I really thought he was the one. Do I believe in the one, or that there is someone who completes me? I used to believe that. What I would see in movies or hear in love songs, I thought that's the kind of love I wanted to experience. But the greatest love story that I know of, that I have experienced for myself, comes only from God. I do believe that from his love he does bring people into our lives to share that love together, so yes in a sense they might be "the one" that God has sent your way, but you should know that you are already complete and made whole by The Almighty One. Your significant other does not complete you. You do not need them to make you happy, that's just a bonus. You also don't need the desire to feel completed by them. I'm going to call you friend because you're reading this book that details my entire life experience, so I feel like it's warranted. Friend, if you don't know your own worth, how do you expect someone else to know?

It started at a young age for me, not feeling loved or wanted by another man. Like I had mentioned before, my parents had me at a young age and unfortunately, they did not end up staying together. I grew up with my mother and we lived with my grandparents for a while before my mom got her own place. I admire how strong she was for both of us and she was so driven. She too had to grow up fast.

I only saw my dad occasionally, and then he joined the Marines. I was so young that I didn't even realize that they were really separated until we moved out of my grandparents' home. I did not have a father figure in the home. I felt there was a huge chapter torn from my book of life, and that was how to truly be loved by a man. I didn't see how a man was really supposed to treat a woman and vice versa. Did my father not love me enough to stay? This, my friend, was the first loss I experienced in my life, and I was only a child.

Of course, I did not fully grasp what was happening, but I knew he was out of the picture. As I got older, I started realizing I was still holding a grudge towards him because let's be honest, who doesn't want to grow up with both of their parents in the home? I know my dad joining the military was hard for me, something I couldn't fully comprehend back then, but I know it was also hard for him to make that type of sacrifice to leave behind loved ones. He needed to support me, even if it was from a distance. They say distance gives us reason to love harder, but I wasn't sure how to fully do that.

I loved and missed my father very much, so when my mother met my step-dad, that was a little harder. As a young child, I did not like the idea of my mom dating another man. I would write him hate letters telling him that I did not like him, and he had to leave us (even at a young age I liked to write). But he didn't leave us, he stayed. They ended up getting married and we moved to yet another small and even hotter desert town in California. I hated my life. I was moving away from my family who I grew up with forever and friends who I thought I was going to graduate with. I was in middle school and thought the world was over! My life sucked.

It took a lot of adjusting, but it was a new season for all of us. My mom and stepdad went through a lot in their marriage. With my mother's permission, I am sharing a little bit of what they experienced because no family or marriage is perfect, and I know I'm not the only one who has been affected by an experience like this. Through these experiences, I was introduced to Jesus and I firmly believe he was constantly watching over us.

My stepfather cheated on my mother. I remember one time my mother picked me up from school and she was crying. She had our bags packed in the car and said we were going back home. My 10-year-old self, of course, was so excited to go back home, but to see my mother so broken sobered the occasion. Why doesn't any man love my mother? Do they not know that when she hurts, I hurt too? I think my middle school season is really the time I started questioning everything.

I am a full believer in second chances. I mean, after all, God gives us a second chance once we fully give our life to him. Actually, through repentance, he gives us multiple chances! I admire my mother's strength when she gave my stepdad another chance. It is through that kind of forgiveness and humility where we really find change within ourselves.

As I got into high school, I experienced my first relationship. His dad and my stepdad were close friends so I would always be around him. He was the tall, dark and handsome guy that all the girls liked, so why did he want to be with me? I was super awkward in high school. I was the brace-faced short girl who was just trying to fit in. I tried fitting in all-too-well, to be honest. I attended high school parties I had no business going to, and I started sneaking out to be with my boyfriend, but at least I had friends, right? As they say, you are the company you keep, but I soon ended up becoming a party of one realizing they weren't really my friends.

I remember having "the talk" once with my mother stating that you don't have sex until you're married and in love. Well, my boyfriend told me he loved me, and we just so happened to be in his room. So, this means I can have sex, right?

Wrong.

Long story short, I lost my virginity. I lost my purity. You could also count this as a loss in my book because it lives with you forever. I felt ashamed and disappointed. But unfortunately, the cycle continued. I slept with other boys who I thought "loved me." It wasn't until I got older that I realized I was trying to fill this void of love because I didn't know how a man should love you.

Let me tell you a story about a woman who was also trying to fill voids of her life by being with men. One day, there was a Samaritan woman gathering water from a well. She noticed a man was sitting by the well she wanted to draw water from. The man had asked her to give him some water since he was tired from traveling. Her being a Samaritan woman and him a Jewish man, she was confused as to why he would even ask this question. He told her, *"Everyone who drinks this water will be thirsty again and again. Anyone who drinks the water I give will never thirst—not ever. The water I give will be an artesian spring within, gushing fountains of endless life." (John 4: 13 MSG).*

So, of course, she asked where do I find this type of water so that I may not have to come to the well again? Instead of answering her question, he told her to go and get her husband, who was in fact not her husband at all. She had five husbands before and now was with a man who was not her husband. She didn't realize that the person she was talking to was in fact, Jesus. The water that she so desperately longed for didn't come from that well or the men in her life, but from Jesus who was the water of eternal life.

In our lives, we tend to go back to this well that may be filled with things that really don't satisfy our thirst. What are you feeding or fueling your soul with? Do you see also that Jesus, not one time labeled her as her past? He only tells us who we really are, not who we used to be.

So, when people start labeling you as something that happened from your past, remember, that's not at all who you are. I would feed my soul with lies from others. Words hurt, for real. *"The tongue can bring death or life; those who love to talk will reap the consequences"* (Proverbs 18:21 NLT). They tend to stick with us for a long period of time, but that's not who I am, and that's not who you are. Most importantly, that's not at all how God sees us.

Our worth does not come from a person. Our worth comes from Jesus. We are made righteous in Jesus. He died for our sins knowing all that was to come. Friend, if God is not going to be enough for you, if you can't see that his love is enough for you, no person ever will be. I did not grow up seeing a healthy relationship. I did not grow up reading the word about relationships.

So, where did I get the idea of relationships from? Movies, songs, things of this broken world. I took pieces of what I thought was love and created my own fairytale. Life is not a Disney fairytale where you wait for prince charming to come and save you. Friend, Jesus is the only one who can save you! We don't need a fairytale to be happy. Be happy with who you are. As a matter of fact, be happy knowing WHOSE you are.

Fast forward 16 years, and I'm happy to say that my mom and stepdad are still together and happily married. Out of their marriage, I got 3 beautiful siblings. They faced extremely hard trials and situations, some that almost ended their marriage, but by the love of God and the love they have for each other, they stuck it out. I'm extremely grateful for my stepdad because he cared for me as his own child. I was never "the stepdaughter", I was his daughter. I'm also extremely grateful and blessed to have my father back in my life. It was a seed in my life that God knew needed watering, and I am happy to say our relationship is blooming beautifully. Although we may never play catchup on the years of the past, God-willing, we have so many more years ahead of us.

To my point, don't let your heart harden over grudges or things of the past you cannot change. You, my friend, are gold. Your heart is pure gold. It may take some time to find it, I surely know it did for me, but when you come to a point where you've just had enough, all you are determined to do is dig for that gold; it's inside us all. God sees your heart as gold, and he is waiting to help you discover it. And when you do, let it shine.

THE SOUREST LEMON

"When a woman is giving birth, she has sorrow because her hour has come, but when she has delivered the baby, she no longer remembers the anguish, for joy that a human being has been born into the world. So also you have sorrow now, but I will see you again, and your hearts will rejoice, and no one will take your joy from you." (John 16: 21-22 ESV).

What Jesus is stating here is that the pain won't last forever. Your sorrow will turn into joy and no one on this earth can take that from you.

How does one cope with the hardest hello and goodbye all at once?

I would like to think I have a high pain tolerance, now more than ever, but on the morning of September 1st, pain wouldn't be enough to describe my experience.

It's 5 am, and all at once, I started to experience the most excruciating contractions ever. *This was it* I thought, *our baby girl is on her way.*

With bags already packed and the room fully decorated, we could not wait to welcome our precious baby girl home. At 6 am, I arrived at the hospital with the help of my grandmother, just 30 minutes away from my home, and the doctors took me back instantly into the room to check on the baby and me. With each painful contraction, I felt I tried to focus on the joy of finally being able to meet this child of ours. They had brought in an ultrasound tech to check on her heartbeat, and I was anxiously waiting to hear that strong and loud heartbeat of hers that I had just heard 3 days before. The doctor slowly walks in behind the nurses, and everything seemed to move in slow motion. That moment became the worst few seconds of my life as piercing words came from the doctor's mouth:

"I'm sorry, but there is no heartbeat."

I don't know what was harder to process at that moment; my heart breaking into a billion pieces, the black screen where my baby girl had laid still, or the weeping sound of my tears and me crying NO over and over again. I tried my best at this moment to not cry loudly because of the other expecting mothers in the room. Most people said I should've cried and yelled at the top of my lungs—and trust me I've had my fair share of times where I've done that—but I just looked up at the white ceiling and let the tears fall down like pouring rain.

It was 7 am, and I was still in shock. I had to make phone calls to family members telling them the news. I don't even know if they understood what I had said, but they could hear the pain in my voice. By 8 am, little by little, people started arriving at the hospital. Their faces were blank. Eyes were red. Others just in complete disbelief. Lost and confused, that's what we were. We all were. I remember the nurse kept asking me if I wanted everyone to leave, but I told her no because if it was just me in the room I would continue to cry hysterically and I was afraid I would never stop.

AJ never left my side. His mother never left my side. My mother never left my side. I was so grateful for the friends and family that did show up that day. I was never alone. Our pastor at the time also came to the hospital and prayed with us. As much as I wanted to believe God was there with us in that moment, I felt he was further away than ever. Have you ever felt that God was not near when you needed him the most? I may not have seen him working in that moment in time, but I know that God constantly works with us.

It had hurt so much to see the look on everyone's faces, but the one face that I will never forget, the one who tried to be strong not just for me, but also for everyone else, was Aria's father. He still had so much hope, hope that somehow, she could still make it, and as he placed his hands on my stomach he just prayed. Even when I had no hope left, he did. I thought he was so strong for that. Here I was just completely hopeless and knew she was already gone forever, but something inside him didn't want to let go. I don't know what he prayed for, but I thought his faith was definitely stronger than mine. I felt like I had failed him. AJ always talked about how much he wanted kids and a family. He had a big loving family, full of beautiful kids. He was great with kids, especially with his nieces and nephews. And here I was, never imagining having kids growing up, to getting pregnant with our first child, to now losing our first child. I can't even begin to tell you the millions of emotions and thoughts running through my mind. At the forefront, though, were two words: *failure* and *disappointment*.

Even more questions ran through my mind: What did I do wrong? Was God punishing me since I didn't want kids growing up? Why did you take her life and not mine? Why me?

I am here today telling you that it's okay to ask these hard questions. God wants us to communicate with him, through the good and the bad.

The Worst Pain

It was almost time to start pushing. I remember reading about how to breathe and push when delivering, but after pushing for hours, I was weak. On top of that, the epidural they gave me didn't even work. I could've done it naturally, but I was already in so much pain. They eventually gave me something stronger which actually knocked me out. Looking back now I barely remember pushing, but I didn't care, because I wanted to feel no pain at all. I couldn't get the thought out of my head knowing that after that final push she would leave me for good, even though her spirit was already in heaven. Moments later, there she was.

After 16 hours of labor and unimaginable pain, around 10 pm on September 1 of 2016, Aria Monet Guinn was born weighing 6 lbs. 13 oz. and was 19 ¼ in. long. Although she was born into our arms, her spirit was already in eternity with Jesus.

Silence filled the room. Her lifeless body lay on my chest. My eyes were captivated by her, but I was in complete shock. I couldn't move nor speak; I was numb. It was like a scene from a movie and the moment where you pray that you never have to experience it, and then it happens to you. She had a head full of beautiful black curls. She looked just like her father. She was literally everything I had prayed for. How I wish I could've looked into her eyes though, to see if they had color. Her father had colored eyes as did his father and my grandmother and my mother, so the odds were pretty good. Either way, I could not see them. What gives me some peace is knowing that when she first opened her beautiful eyes, she got to see Jesus.

She looked so fragile. They dressed her in clothes we had picked out for her to wear to go home. I even had bought us matching outfits, but so much for that. Groups of 3-4 people started coming in to meet her. It was hard to look at everyone's reactions. God, this is not what I had envisioned. No one was making cute baby noises at her or saying how cute she looked. Nothing but pure silence. I wanted to hear her cry. I wanted to hear people go back and forth on who she looked like more. I wanted to hear anything but silence. I held her in my arms and just stared at her face. There was bruising all around her and I remember blood started coming out of her nose once her father took her. Unfortunately, we couldn't have her to ourselves that much longer because her body had no oxygen. I wasn't ready to let her go, but I had to.

One thing I remember vividly though is that I had the best nurses, hands down. They ended up moving me into another room just so I didn't have to hear other crying babies or mothers giving birth. A pretty box with ribbon was delivered to us, and inside was a note from all the nurses with their condolences as well as some baby clothes and a lock of her hair. My mother wanted to take pictures and from those pictures, she created a photo album for the box. Honestly, I hated that box. To think that every time I opened it, it would just remind me of horrible memories. To think that every time I wanted to "see" my daughter I would have to open a box or flip through pages? No thank you.

I didn't want to leave the hospital because I knew that once I left, reality would hit, and it would hurt like hell. And it did, if not more. The nurses came in with a stroller and once I sat in it, I started bawling. I envisioned being strolled out with my baby girl and beautiful balloons to go along with it. A little parade of just the two of us, but it was only me. They strolled me outside where my dad picked me up. He had just flown in from North Carolina the day before. He literally got the next plane ticket to come out and be with me. Unfortunately, he came right after I had her, so he didn't get to meet his granddaughter. This picture didn't feel right. I was leaving the hospital empty-handed. I was going home alone.

An empty crib that was meant to hold our baby girl, an empty heart that was supposed to be filled with joy. Lord, all of this, for what, nothing? A piece of me was gone. A piece of me that I knew could never be fixed or replaced. Plans changed, life changed, my whole world around me changed. My views and outlook on life changed, my heart changed. I wish I could say that it got easier, but it did not. It got harder.

It took me many months to not be angry with God for taking her away from me. How could He possibly let me carry her for 9 months and then be left with nothing for the rest of my life? How does God expect me to handle this? You know that phrase, "God wouldn't give you more than you could handle"? Well, how the heck was I supposed to handle this. I am guilty of once having this type of mindset. I get it, people try to give you advice and they mean well, but honestly, don't give advice on a topic you have no experience or expertise on. God doesn't want us to go through hard times. He especially doesn't want us to go through these times alone. Unfortunately, we live in a broken world where the unimaginable and the unfathomable things do happen. Fortunately, this world is not our forever home.

It took me a while to talk about the loss of Aria, but I am not afraid anymore. Does it still make my heart beat a thousand times faster and make my body quiver when someone new asks me about Aria? For sure. My hands might even sweat a little, and my stomach might be in knots the size of a rollercoaster, but it allows me to not only continue to talk about her but to also talk about the love and sweet grace of God.

Grieving

> "Grief, I've learned, is really just love. It's all the love you want to give but cannot. All that unspent love gathers up in the corners of your eyes, the lump in your throat, and in that hallow part of your chest. Grief is just love with no place to go."
>
> —Jamie Anderson

A Life After Loss

"Give it time" or "it will pass", are some of the phrases I'd hear about grieving. Grieving is a process. I do not believe that there is a timeline nor deadline for when one should stop, if ever. Everyone heals and grieves differently. I admit wholeheartedly that even four years later I grieve and mourn the loss of my baby girl. Does it hurt as bad the first time? Not entirely. Do the memories and pain still come as they please? Yes. My eyes still puff up and become piercing red circles. Tears still stream down my face. My heart still mourns her loss and I still miss her deeply. I always will miss her.

For the first few months, it was hard for me to even see a child, let alone a newborn baby. I remember watching a show with AJ and when a scene came up with a baby crying, he got up and turned it off. Yes, it was that hard for me to hear another baby's cry because I did not get to hear her cry. I wondered how she may have sounded. I wondered many, many things about how she would have been if she were still here. I felt like a fool for feeling this way, but I did not know how else to feel. I had no one close to me to talk to who has grieved the way I was grieving.

My time with God drifted away because my time was spent on hopeless wonders and what-ifs. Not only did my time with God dwindle, but so did my time with others. It's like I had put these walls up to avoid any more hurt. I didn't realize those walls were also hurting others. The stages of grief are real, and I felt like I visited them over and over again.

I was in denial all over again. It's like my mind and body automatically switch to defense mode. Maybe the doctors can save her. Maybe God will deliver us a miracle. Maybe we will hear her heartbeat once again. There was no point in me trying to be optimistic, but I still tried to believe in the maybe.

I knew the second stage far too well—anger. I was angry with God even when I did not want to be. I was angry for him taking away our baby girl too soon. He took away my dream school and now being a mom? Why would he let me be a mom for all those months and then just decide that I should not be one? I was also angry with myself, which led to the next stage: bargaining. If only I had paid more attention to her kicks. If only I had been with her father just the night before. If only I had used the right products and ate the right foods. If only.

Part 2: The Sourest Lemon

When the stage of depression came, I finally visited a counselor. I just didn't know how to cope on an emotional or mental level. Even if I was talking to someone who had no idea what I was going through, at least I was talking about it and talking about her. I couldn't seem to find my purpose. What is the purpose of a loss? How does God expect me to just move on? I could never imagine a life without her, and now I was actually living in it. I did not want to accept this new life that God had for me, for all of us.

I knew if I could not accept it, I would not go anywhere. I would be trapped in the hopeless wonders and what-ifs that were just fantasy. I had to accept the fact that I was a mother, even if I had no proof of it here on earth. I had to accept the fact that God did not do this to hurt us. But I couldn't accept these facts, at least not all at once.

Romans 8:28 (ESV) states, *"And we know that for those who love God all things work together for good, for those who are called according to his purpose."* I knew I loved God and that he only wanted good for me, but was there really a way to turn this pain into purpose? What was his purpose for me?

March For Babies

"1 in 4 pregnancies end in a loss."[1]

Aria's father and I got tattoos in honor of her after her passing. The placement of mine was done on the right inside of my wrist saying, Aria Monet. Most people don't notice it, or if they do, they don't ask about it. I can count on one hand the number of people who have actually asked me what my tattoo meant, without me telling them the backstory. I had a coworker once ask me if it was French and I explained that it was not. Going back to work after losing Aria was the absolute hardest thing out of all the absolute hardest things I had already experienced. It was going back to reality but putting on a poker face. I was running away from anyone who wanted to hug me. I ran away into my car on my lunch break to cry because I just wasn't ready to open up about

---

1. "Stillbirth," *March of Dimes.* https://www.marchofdimes.org/complications/stillbirth.aspx"1 In 4 Pregnancies, Not 1 in 4 Women," *Don't Talk About the Baby.* https://www.donttalkaboutthebaby.com/single-post/2016/05/24/1-in-4-pregnancies-not-1-in-4-women-1

it. How I look back on those times now and just thank God for being there for me, even when I couldn't feel or see it.

Back to my coworker's question. He then asked me what my tattoo meant, and I shortly responded back that it was my daughter's name. He was shocked since he didn't know I had a daughter and never spoke about her, and then asked how old she was. Clearing my throat, I told him that she was stillborn. My eyes were starting to get teary as he asked me what a stillbirth was. I could see that he was serious, so I told him in the easiest and hardest way possible, that she was born not breathing. It was a little shocking to me honestly that there were people out there who really didn't know what stillbirth was. It is also shocking that there are people out there who have never tried coffee, but that's a different story. This was a moment where I knew I wanted to break the silence. The next time someone asked me what my tattoo meant, I wouldn't feel as scared as before. It not only lets me still talk about her like she is still here, but it also lets me talk about Jesus. I can now say with a little bit of ease, that she is with Jesus in heaven, and they have both saved me.

In April of 2018, God gave me that opportunity to break that silence about stillbirth. This is where I felt I could take that first step towards turning my pain into purpose. AJ and I were chosen to be the ambassador family of the high desert for the March of Dimes. For those who do not know what the March of Dimes is, it is a non-profit organization that fights for the health of all mothers and babies. This organization is incredible. I'm not just saying this because we were chosen to be the ambassador family, but because I had the privilege to also be an intern for the organization for a few months and was able to see the work they do behind the scenes.

A Life After Loss

I put my time and dedication into this organization because I truly wanted to help others who were fighting for themselves and their babies. It was an eye-opener for sure. I would make phone calls to families and hear their stories and remember how crazy it was that some of them have never even shared them before. Before I would leave to go back home, I remember sometimes crying in my car. Little did they know that on the other side of the phone line I, too, was going through a difficult time. God knew I was going to be there, but I did not. God knew I was going to help others get through this, but I did not.

Through the organization, I made a new friend and met a mother who also went through not one loss, but multiple losses. She was also the previous year's ambassador family. One day we met up for coffee and I simply asked her, how did you do it? I couldn't get over her admirable faith and strength in God, and how that one day she and her husband would have a child again. Fast forward to several years later, and I'm happy to say that they did. Her faith in God gave me some confidence that maybe one day it will also be in the books for me.

The day came where we would walk for those babies fighting for their lives and for those whose lives were already taken. Our families had designed cute shirts that said, "Team Aria Guinn" with a heart and footprints on the front, and on the back, it had her birthday with handprints. My hands were extremely sweaty before giving my speech. I remember when they told me I had to give a speech I was a little hesitant. I mean, of course, I wanted to talk about my baby girl, but I had literally just lost her. What if no one even cares? What if people judge me for my age? Here come all the negative questions rolling in.

I decided to do it because I wanted to break the silence of stillbirth. I decided to do it for all the other mothers who had no voice. Most importantly, I decided to do it for myself. It was healing I never knew I needed. It wasn't for publicity, but for the fact that I got to talk about my baby girl. Much so like I am doing now.

I gave my speech to over five hundred people that day. I paused a few times to catch my breath, but I did it and had the best support system ever. A stranger came up to me afterward and just hugged me. At first, I thought it was weird, but also thought it was kind of amazing. They didn't even say anything, but just hugged me.

Sometimes we think we always need to have a response to a situation, but sometimes silence is the best response. If we haven't been through the same situation as someone, sometimes just showing up and being there for them is enough. I'm not saying that you have to go out and give a speech to hundreds of people, but if sharing your story with even just one person can lighten the weight on your heart, share it. You never know who may need to hear it.

One day at the hospital, after I had given birth to Aria, I remember the doctor asking me how far along I was since my stomach was still big. I went into detail about what had happened and found out that he and his wife also lost a child due to stillbirth. "Stillbirth is when a baby dies in the womb after 20 weeks of pregnancy. Most stillbirths happen before a woman goes into labor, but a small number happen during labor and birth. Stillbirth affects about 1 in 160 pregnancies each year in the United States; this is about 1 percent of all pregnancies and about 24,000 babies."[1]

Miscarriage, ectopic pregnancy, stillbirth, whatever your loss may be, it hurts. Any type of loss hurts, and it hurts like hell, but God doesn't waste our hurt or pain. I've learned that you don't have to hide your pain or wear your pain. If you embrace your pain, you can then share it with God and share it with others. You can talk about your baby. You can talk about how precious your time was with them and be honest with how it felt when your time was up. You can talk about your pain and know that you don't have to deal with it alone.

Tis the Season

The most wonderful time of the year is also one of the hardest times of the year for me. There's not a single day, holiday, or family event that I don't wish Aria was with us. I remember one of the gifts someone had bought us was a beautiful red gown for her to wear for Christmas. I ended up giving the gown away, but as I did, I tried to visually picture her in it. Her beautiful curly hair with a bedazzled hair bow, and glittery black slippers. Us taking family photos and sending out Christmas and happy new year cards. That was not meant to be.

My heart longed for all the family things. My heart still has a longing for it. The first Christmas without her my aunt had bought a beautiful ornament with her name on it and another with angel wings and her birthday. My mother had also bought one with her name on it for her tree and I remember she had another one that said, Jesus. I decided to put her name right next to the one that said Jesus to remind me that they were together, side by side in heaven.

All I wanted for Christmas was her. Just to hold her again in my arms, but this time for a little bit longer. Time can be the worst kind of friend. It's there when you need it and then gone in a second. I've also learned that time cannot be controlled; as much as we think we can try to control our time, we simply cannot. We can manage our time or waste our time. We can value our time or lose time. What we cannot control is our time here on earth.

Ecclesiastes 3:11 (ESV) states that *"He has made everything beautiful in its time. Also, he has put eternity into man's heart, yet so that he cannot find out what God has done from the beginning to end."* If we knew what was going to happen to us before it even came into existence, would we still choose that same path or go on another route? Of course, we would always pick the path that looks better or looks like it is the easiest or even the shortest route. But maybe, just maybe, God wants us to go on another route. One that may take longer but has more purpose. *"It is in Christ that we find out who we are and what we are living for."* (Ephesians 1:11-12 MSG). Maybe, just maybe, what God has for us during a certain season is necessary for us to experience because if God has led you to it, he will lead you through it.

Part 3:

A HARDEN HEART

"The heart is hopelessly dark and deceitful, a puzzle that no one can figure out. But I, God, search the heart and examine the mind. I get to the heart of a human. I get to the root of things. I treat them as they really are, not as they pretend to be." (Jeremiah 17:10 MSG).

The heart really is like a puzzle. There are pieces even we can't figure out or are still trying to find. But when God has the pieces, he creates the most beautiful masterpiece.

My days got longer and lonelier. I had loved ones all around me, but still felt like I was in some other world. My heart felt like it broke into a billion pieces. Did you know that broken heart syndrome is a thing? It's caused by intense emotional or physical stress which can weaken the heart muscle. I'm no doctor, but if I was able to diagnose myself, I'd say I've experienced that, and then some.

Speaking of doctors, they took multiple tests on both Aria and me but could not determine what had caused her death. They gave us another option, which would have cost thousands of dollars, and that was to do an autopsy on her body. My instant thought was no way! I couldn't begin to fathom the thought or even begin to try to visualize them cutting open my baby girl. But

I decided to at least email the people to see what they would say and thankfully, they were honest and stated that about 90% of the work they do on young babies, there is nothing wrong with them. So, to not only save money but to also have a sane mind that our baby girl wasn't going to get opened up, we decided to not do it. People ask me if I ever wish I "knew" what happened or if I would have gone through with the autopsy, but I am okay with saying I left that up to God.

Hurt People, Hurt People

I told myself, "No one is going to love someone as broken as me." But I was wrong. Just days after losing our daughter, AJ had proposed to me and I said yes. Honestly, when I saw the ring I was in complete shock. We had mentioned marriage before, (remember the promise ring too), but that wasn't even a thought for me anymore after what had happened. I knew this man wanted kids, a wife, and a family. In my mind, I thought he must really love me if even after all this he still wants to spend the rest of his days with me.

We were engaged for a year, and during that time we still experienced bumps in the road. There were red flags waving both ways, but we ignored them and still pursued a wedding. I had lived with my grandparents while we were engaged and him with his parents. I wish I could say that the loss of our daughter was the reason why we grew more distant, and although I have to say for myself it is one of the biggest factors for sure, it simply was not the only reason.

On September 16th, 2017, we said I do and became officially married. Afterward, I moved in with him and his family. I remember before we got married his mother had asked me why we chose to be married in September. We didn't meet until December and he asked me out in January, so why September? My response was, "Too much bad had happened in September. I wanted to celebrate something good." It was supposed to be something so good and beautiful that nothing could sever it, but it instead became something atrocious.

Everyone has their breaking point, a limit to where they've just had enough. My breaking point happened on an evening I would never forget. I yelled at people and my emotions ran wild. That evening AJ and I, as well as some family members and friends, had all went out for dancing and drinks, but

Part 3: A Harden Heart

I was not in the mood. To others, I probably never seemed like I was in the mood to do anything. Writing this now is actually hard for me because anyone who truly knows me knows that wasn't the real me at all. It's sad looking back at the girl I used to be. But thank God I am not her anymore. Thank God that the only time I look back now is to see how far I have come. Do you ever tend to catch yourself having flashbacks of the old you? Sometimes it can be a real eye-opener.

I love dancing and danced all throughout high school, but I was a party pooper this night and decided I did not want to join in on the fun at all. As we were leaving, a conversation was brought up involving babies and birth choices, which I was not aware of, and I was in disbelief. During the drive back home I thought to myself, why would they be talking about this in front of me knowing good and well what I just went through?

Well, that's when the abrupt words came from my mouth. I yelled and told them to stop talking about it. At this moment my husband's brother, his brother's fiancé, and friend got out of the car and walked the rest of the way home. AJ was disappointed in me, and the evening turned into my worst nightmare. Words were exchanged amongst others and the truth about us deciding to separate finally came out. I voiced my opinion a lot about getting a divorce, but it's something I never really sat down to discuss with him. I would just toss it around like a penny floating in the air thinking it was just this easy thing to throw around, but it cost us a lot.

Later that evening we drove to my grandparents to stay the night there so that we could give everyone some space. We all lived together so we were hoping that the tension would ease returning in the morning. I remember lying next to him and seeing how disappointed he was in me. I never wanted to get between anyone, especially not anyone in his family. I didn't want to be that girl, but there I was.

This, my friend, was my breaking point. I knew I had to do something; a text message saying sorry wouldn't suffice. I wanted to try and fix everything so quickly, but the thing with big messes, especially ones that you have made, is that if you try to clean it up too quickly, you might just make it worse or leave a stain. So, to avoid any bigger messes, I took a getaway trip to visit my family in North Carolina. I was with them for about a week and during that time I had talked with AJ, his sister, and his brother's fiancé. I made some big decisions during that time, like removing myself from his brother's and fiancé's bridal party, and also deciding to move out. I had to pull myself together, and I knew I couldn't do it there.

I was feeling down, hurt, depressed, and was also bringing people down around me. The only thing I knew I could do was to leave. I used to do that a lot actually. You ever just run away from a problem acting like it's not there, or just sweep it under the rug? Well, eventually that problem is going to come out, and maybe even worse than it was before.

I still remember so vividly the day of me getting my things together and moving out of his parent's house. I had my cousin help me move out because I couldn't face AJ or his family alone. To make things even harder for me, almost everyone was home, except him. Was he not home because he would have wanted to stop me? Or was he not home because it would be hard for him to watch me leave and do nothing? This was my decision though, and I knew it had to be done.

Once I moved back in with my grandparents, I tried figuring how to be this picture-perfect wife, daughter-in-law, sister-in-law, etc. All these different hats I had to figure out how to wear. I even bought marriage books trying to seek some guidance on what to do. There would be nights where I would go back and stay with him, but it wouldn't be the same. It was too late.

Six months later we filed for a divorce. I received the divorce finalization on Christmas Eve. What a time to receive them, I thought. Holidays were already a tough time, but that year they were a little tougher. This was the third hardest loss of my life. So now I guess the month of September holds many losses, but I have learned and grown so much from it. I acknowledge now more than ever that I was not in the right head or heart space to fully love someone like they deserved to be loved. I remember telling AJ's sister, "How can I love your brother when I don't even love myself?"

I was far from myself, whoever that was. My heart was truly hardened. I started thinking about my own feelings rather than those around me. I felt I was alone in this loss, and I didn't even acknowledge that AJ, too, had lost her. I was so caught up in my own emotions and rarely saw his. Was it just because he was good at hiding it or that he didn't want to speak about it as much as I did? I don't know. We both grieved differently, and at the time I didn't understand how or why, but I do now. I understand now that it was okay that we grieved differently as long as we did it together, but we did not.

Never have I ever thought I'd experience grief so hard again. This type of lifestyle almost seemed inevitable. The pain and grief just weighed more and more on my chest as I now experienced the loss of two loves. I won't go into every stage of grief like I did when we lost our daughter, but it was the kind of loss that hits your core and leaves you out of breath.

What I realize now is that during that time I did not seek out God enough for our marriage. Although the marriage books and counseling gave me some insight, nothing is more crystal clear than God's word. If only I knew then what I know now. As cliché as that sounds, it is so true. Do I wish we were still together? I actually got asked this question a lot and still do get asked this question sometimes. My answer, though, is no. We were not healthy individuals. We went through something that no one should ever go through and then we added a marriage on top of it. Marriage isn't a band-aid for any matter. And like any other relationship, there were issues that had not been resolved. We still had a lot of growing to do, and unfortunately, that growth was not together.

Should a married couple grow through hard times? Absolutely. Marriage is a life-long, beautiful commitment that I one day hope to fully experience. But only healthy individuals make a healthy marriage, and healthy I was not. My heart was not in a healthy state to love as it should. It felt like my heart was the size of a fairy fly (which is a type of wasp by the way), and theirs is the smallest heart of all living creatures. Yeah, it felt that small. That's the type of heart I felt I had.

I will always have a love for Aria's father; without him, I wouldn't be the mother I am today. I wish him nothing but the best and I appreciate all that he has done for me as well as his family. They will always be a huge part of my life even though they are no longer in it.

They say divorce is worse than death, and that God hates divorce, but I beg to differ. Maybe it's because I didn't get to fully experience what life was like as a married couple, having our own place and truly growing together, but either way, nothing topped the loss of our daughter. Maybe God does hate divorce, and for that, I have asked for forgiveness. I've come to find that even through our own wrongdoings, God still has a way for us. He doesn't turn his back on us; he wants to be there for us.

I still felt like I had failed at everything God placed in my life. I couldn't be a mom or a wife, and therefore I could never have a family of my own. These were the lies the enemy wanted me to believe. These lies consumed my life for quite some time. During my alone time, though, I have grown so much closer with God and I realized that those lies do not define me. One day, God willing, I will have those things again. And although I don't have a child physically on earth, I'll always be a mom and have that motherly love in my heart. If you have experienced a miscarriage, stillborn, or any loss of a child, you are still a mom. You are still a father. You are still a parent. You just have an angel child now.

It's Okay to Not Be Okay

The plus side of moving back in with my grandparents was that there was always coffee ready in the morning. God bless my grandparents and their love for caffeine. One morning while having coffee with my grandmother, she said, "You lost your daughter and husband both in a matter of 2 years. How are you going to handle that?" That question really got me thinking. I never looked at it that way before until she said something. I kept stirring my hot coffee while looking at the creamer swirl around in the mug. My mind was just swirling around, not going anywhere but in a circle. With a loud sigh, I stated, "I don't know."

And I was not okay with that answer.

How is one ever to handle a loss, let alone two? I figured maybe it was my fault and all my doing. I couldn't even talk to God because of how disappointed I was in myself. You know what though? God doesn't see us as our failures or our sins. He sees us as we truly are, his children. As any child would be afraid to talk with a parent after doing something wrong, God wants us to still talk to him. He wants us to know that it is okay to not be okay because as long as we have him, it will be okay in the end.

We don't always need a quick response to a question. Especially one like my grandmother asked. If you give someone false information, you're only kidding yourself. It's okay to not know right away how you are going to handle a situation. The only thing you can do, and what worked for me, is to ask God to help change your "I don't know" into an "I don't know, but...".

"I don't know, but I know God will lead me through it."

Friend, if he has brought you to it, he will bring you through it. Easier said than done right? He knows your past, your present, and your future. So, he knows. He knows every "I don't know" we will say to a question, but best believe he will be providing you a way to a definite answer.

I said before that no one is going to love someone so broken. But I was wrong.

God loves me and he loves you. It's the best kind of love there is. God has picked each and every one of those broken pieces of your heart scattered all over the floor to delicately form them into something far greater than our minds can ever imagine. Give him all of your heart. God doesn't give only a part of his heart, so why should we?

Part 4:

THROUGH THE STORM

"Even though I walk through the valley of the shadow of death,
I will fear no evil, for you are with me; your rod and your staff,
they comfort me." (Psalm 23:4 ESV).

In any scary situation, no matter how big or small the storm, I know this verse will give me comfort. I hope it does the same for you.

ever would I ever have thought about experiencing Posttraumatic Stress Disorder. My experience of PTSD in the evenings was frightening. I would dream about that black screen in the hospital where my baby girl's face was still and lifeless. The dreams were all too surreal and scary to the point where I'd just wake up panting. It was like my own hell, and I was constantly reliving it over and over again. Stepping into that hospital again was a definite no for me or any hospital ever. Being around anything that was baby-related, or ultrasound-related, took a toll on me.

I never really mentioned it to anyone because I didn't want people to think I was crazy, or maybe crazier. To this day, that image is forever ingrained in my mind. What does one do when they can't control their own thoughts, let alone their own dreams? Well, you can control them. It takes practice, but with time and guidance, mine specifically from God, you get better. The dreams and thoughts will become less daunting, and you will replace them with dreams and thoughts that are more comforting.

One thing I wish I could've done more was dream of her. It's like my heart and mind tried connecting together to create dreams that should've been reality: birthday parties, her first walk, her first words, but it's also like my heart and mind didn't want to disappoint me. I remember one day receiving a text from my mother about how she had a dream about Aria: *"I had a dream of a beautiful lady statue who came to life with beautiful white butterflies all around and I was chasing them, crying looking for Aria. I found her so beautiful, the prettiest eyes, so light complexion with curly short hair. I couldn't touch her, but she was so happy."* Let me tell you, my eyes were piercing red after reading this text message because she had a beautiful vivid dream of what Aria looked like, and then the last part, *but she was so happy.*

If anything calms my heart and soul more, it's knowing that she is so happy. There's not a day that goes by that I don't wish she was here with us to be happy, but to know that she is in heaven with her heavenly Father brings the uttermost joy to my heart. After the conversation I had with my mother, I decided to look up what her dream meant. Have you ever had a dream where you're like well, what does this mean? It wasn't my dream, but I decided to look up several articles online to find the meaning of my mother's dream. The most captivating one I found out was that the white butterfly symbolized a sign from heaven. (Insert mind-blown emoji). Was this article 100% accurate? Who knows, but to me, it just confirmed that Aria is indeed thinking of us, too. Every time I see a butterfly I just smile now. Not because I think it's my baby girl, but to really think of what the butterfly represents. *Therefore, if anyone is in Christ, he is a new creation. The old has passed away; behold, the new has come.* (2 Corinthians 5:17 ESV). A butterfly was first a caterpillar before it began to transform into this beautiful new creation. Aria represents this beautiful transformation of once being a little loving nugget in my womb to now spreading her wings high in heaven.

Baby Land

There is death, and then there is sudden death. Some already may see it coming while others don't. For instance, someone being diagnosed with cancer versus someone being in an accident. While both are extremely tragic and hurt like hell, there's just something about sudden death that hits you in your core, drops you to your knees, and makes you gasp heavily for air. And the worst part, you don't see it coming and are not prepared for it. Is one ever ready to experience a loss so heavy?

I remember before I even gave birth to Aria a social worker came in providing us with a binder filled with different counselors and gravesites. In my mind, I wanted to do nothing more than to grab that binder and toss it in the trash. We haven't even had the chance to see our daughter and you're already coming in here with this? Seriously? I knew people around us just wanted to help, and I also knew it's something we had to do, but I did not want to.

I remember looking through the pamphlets and trying to envision where I would lay her to rest. I was already planning a funeral before she was even brought into this world. What kind of life is this? There was one place that stood out to me though amongst all the others. The pictures looked beautiful, and I thought that's where she should be.

The day finally came where we had to go and pick out a casket, a headstone, what the headstone would say, and what location she would be laid to rest. When AJ and I finally got there, I remember just sitting in the room looking at all the papers and just hysterically crying. At this point in time, there was no more trying to hold it all together. Again, I was eternally grateful that AJ was by my side, as well as our mothers, because I could not picture doing this on my own, let alone doing it at all.

We were blessed to receive money to help cover the funeral costs from family, friends, and even strangers. Even for a small baby's funeral, it was still expensive. They specifically had a place called baby land where all children were in one spot together. How beautiful, yet so sad. Looking at the other headstones I tried to find some peace knowing that my little girl was not the only baby up there. There were other parents out there who went through the same thing we were going through, burying a child.

No parent should ever endure such pain or loss. No parent should ever have to fathom the stress of trying to plan a funeral. Unfortunately, we live in a world where there is death. Fortunately, there is an eternal life waiting for us. I pray that whenever you feel that mourning of your child, that you remember that one day you will be with them again for eternity.

A Life After Loss

As I mentioned before, the month of September is very hard for me. I lost my daughter, we laid her to rest, and it was the month I had gotten married. Now, not having a daughter on earth, and not being married, I usually take a vacation around this time for my emotional and spiritual health. I use this time to be surrounded by loved ones and ensure I also have more quiet time with God because only he knows how I really feel. I highly encourage a weekend getaway for yourself or even with a loved one to just refresh your soul.

On September 23, 2016, we laid our baby girl to rest. This was the second hardest day of my life, the first being the day we lost her. I was only 21 years old and had already experienced a loss that most people never had. Fast forward four years later and here I am writing this book. I just celebrated my 25th birthday and most people say I have yet to experience life and should wait to write a book until I'm older. Well, I'm here today to tell you that God does not put a limit on age.

Have you heard of David and Goliath? Well long story short, David was a young boy already facing giants! He defeated Goliath knowing that God was with him. Have you ever heard of Timothy? He was a young pastor who Paul calls his "son in the faith" and he helped spread the good news, despite the hardships he may have had along the way. His job was to "fight the good fight". It does not matter your age, your sex, or race when you do what God has called you to do. No matter how big or small it may be, if it has been weighing heavily on your heart, pray about it and then go work on what you just prayed for.

Rewind back to September 23rd. I do have to say it was a beautiful service. When we first walked into the room, I glanced at the casket and the people in the room and almost dropped down to my knees. It was like this huge wave of reality without her just hit, and it hit hard. Her casket was so small and beautiful. There were beautiful pink roses all around her and a cute white teddy bear. I couldn't get the vision out of my head that our baby girl was in there.

A family friend from Nevada had bought two beautiful white dresses for Aria that were made from old wedding dresses. It was a stunning dress, but still, the thought of not actually seeing her in it was heartbreaking. We picked one out for her to wear and told the funeral staff to keep the other for another family to give to their angel baby. I saw no need to keep it, so I passed it on. I'm sure our angel babies looked beautiful in them.

I remember the pastor had mentioned what the meaning of Aria's name was. Her first name Aria meaning melody, or lion of God. Her middle name Monet meaning to be heard. I was absolutely amazed and had no idea. Hear her roar. A melody to be heard. Her purpose in heaven was far greater than that of earth. And although she was not here on earth, she still touched the hearts of many.

It was our turn to go up and speak, but the only thing I managed to do was cry an ocean of tears. I scanned the room gradually while looking at everyone's faces. My dearest siblings, only ten and twelve years of age already experiencing a loss so heavy they couldn't fathom. Their first niece and they didn't even get to meet her. My loving parents, first-time grandparents, but to an angel baby. My sweetest in-laws, this was not how I envisioned welcoming AJ and I's first child into the family, oh how I felt like I failed them. I wish I could have said one thing, just one thing, but I did not. Thankfully AJ was strong enough to at least say thank you to everyone for coming. After that, we went to take her to baby land.

Family and friends from afar gathered with us that day. One family member in particular though was one of the hardest to see, and that was my cousin's little baby boy who was just born a few weeks before Aria. She and I got to experience being pregnant together and it was amazing! I got to go to her baby shower and she got to go to mine. Funny story, we even had an old photo of us in high school of us having balloons in our shirts "pretending" that we were pregnant. It was destined that one day it was going to happen, and it actually did! We were both extremely excited that our kids were going to be the best of friends, and then there they were, finally together, but not in a way we could've ever fathomed. Honestly, it was so hard for me to even hold her son at first. My heart definitely dropped into my stomach. I felt guilty for feeling this way, but what I had pictured in my mind of when they first met was me holding him and her holding Aria. But one of us was empty-handed. Four years later, I'm happy to say that I have had the opportunity and privilege of watching him grow into a beautiful little boy, and I know that Aria and he for sure would've been the best of buds.

This was the hardest and most unprepared goodbye ever. Some people think going to a gravesite to sit or talk to a loved one is insane. Some people look at it as it's only a headstone or it's only their body. Although there is some truth behind that, there is absolutely nothing wrong with it.

Everyone grieves differently and everyone heals differently. No one should ever make you feel like you are not grieving or healing properly if they themselves have not been in your shoes. Most importantly though, don't do the healing alone. By this, I mean ask God to heal you. If you haven't experienced a relationship with God, seek guidance or help from loved ones or even counseling. I am only here to tell you my personal experience of healing, and that true healing only came from having a relationship with God. He is there when you are at your lowest low. He is there when you are crying throughout the night. He is there to wipe away your tears. He is always there. *"You keep track of all my sorrows. You have collected all my tears in your bottle. You have recorded each one in your book."* (Psalm 56:8 NLT).

Drop the Baggage

You would think that after burying your own child you would feel some type of closure, right? Not me. I continued on with my life, but I was carrying around all this weight of loss, disappointment, hurt, and shame. This was no way of living and I felt it physically weighing down on my heart. Thankfully God has sent me great friends to talk with whenever I needed to just vent. One of my dearest friends who I have had the pleasure of being friends with since high school once told me, "You can't hold on to baggage and try to move forward at the same time." My clever and wonderful friend was right. I could not move on with my life if all I was trying to do was carry all this weight on my own. So, I had two options. I could either continue to carry it and just be stuck and content with where I was, or I could drop the baggage and give it to God. I picked option number two.

I told myself: "Lord, I'm leaving all my baggage with you; no matter the load, I will not pick it up again." Life isn't always fair or easy, so I know that there will be more times where we feel like there's too much on our plate or that our baggage has yet again returned into our hands. When those times do come, pray that God will graciously take them from your hands and give you rest. *"Come to me, all who labor and are heavy laden, and I will give you rest. Take my yoke upon you, and learn from me, for I am gentle and lowly in heart, and you will find rest for your souls. For my yoke is easy, and my burden is light." (Matthew 11:28-30 ESV).*

So, how do you get through the storm? Do you pray during the storm or do you merely wallow in it watching it grow and grow? When storms come raging in it can be overwhelming, but my God is so overwhelmingly powerful, and he is Almighty! We don't let the storm get all of our attention. Just like a tornado twirling vastly damaging a whole town, it will damage our soul. Through the storm, we continually give our attention over to God, because only he can calm it and tell it to, be still. *"Jesus responded, "Why are you afraid? You have so little faith!" Then he got up and rebuked the wind and waves, and suddenly there was a great calm." (Matthew 8:26 NLT).* Remember, you aren't alone in this storm.

Part 5:

ROCK BOTTOM

"And after you have suffered a little while, the God of all grace, who has called you to his eternal glory in Christ, will himself restore, confirm, strengthen and establish you." (1 Peter 5:20 ESV).

Restoration is available for everyone. God's grace is always there. There's a strength inside of you that needs to be awakened.

emember how I talked about the three hardest losses in my life? The loss of a father figure at a young age, the loss of my daughter, and my marriage. Well, there was almost a fourth: my own life. I contemplated sharing this part of my life with others because it is so fragile. Here I am, though, pouring my heart and soul into this book because I want you to know that I am not perfect. Just because I have a relationship with Jesus does not mean that all my days are rainbows and butterflies. It is okay to still go through things like anxiety and depression because we live in a broken world that is not whole. Jesus knows that this world will never be whole. This is why he died for our sins and so that we may have a relationship with him.

Have you ever seen or heard of the popular TV show *The Vampire Diaries?* Well, the vampires in this series have the ability to turn off their "humanity switch". If they turn off their humanity switch, they feel absolutely zero emotion or pain. They become numb, careless, and reckless. If that was an option for me, I'd do it in a heartbeat. Let me be real with you here. Suicidal thoughts are real, and they can be vicious. If you are having suicidal thoughts, I hope that you will seek help.

If I have learned anything, it's that these thoughts are a picture of your emotions warped up into one big lie that tells you that you are not enough, but you are enough. It's a lie that tells you that you can't get through the pain, but you can. It's a lie that people won't miss you, but they will. You might be thinking, well you don't how I feel or what I've gone through, and for that thought, you are one hundred percent correct. What I am saying is that your feelings are valid, but they should not be stored away where they can continue to pile up inside you because once these feelings inside you continue to be turned away, they will consume you.

The Pit

One night I almost drank my life away. Drop by drop, I was trying to let go of the pain. The alcohol consumed every bit of emotion I was feeling that evening. Goodbye to the feelings of being a failure, goodbye to the feelings of hopelessness, goodbye to the feelings of love.

It was one of the coldest nights alone, and by cold, I don't just mean the weather. I have what's called a non-alcoholic fatty liver disease (NAFLD). I found this out when I was only fourteen. Basically, my liver consumes all the bad fats I eat or drink, and if I were to drink too much, well, it could fail. It may not have been the quickest way to let my life go, but it was the only way I knew to numb to the pain. I was broken. I was alone. While lying on my back on the floor, I cried for all I had lost. I cried for the girl who had such big dreams. I cried for the girl who had lost her way and was now at the bottom of a pit and felt there was no way out.

I cried so loud that it felt like all my cries were echoing and talking to each other. I think they were talking to someone though. As I was lying on the floor, random images in my mind started to form. They were images of my family and friends; images of the love I had around me; images of how far I've come. I prayed and thanked God for bringing those images to life. They weren't hallucinations, they were memories. Moments of life I would never forget. At that moment, I knew I had so many more to make.

Part 5: Rock Bottom

I had to start getting out of that pit, but I couldn't do it alone. Friend, there is no pit too dark or too deep that God cannot reach. He reached mine, and I know he can reach yours. I continued going to counseling, a Christian counselor, for my own mental and spiritual sanity. I remember telling the counselor about these thoughts I had about taking my own life. What I felt about being a failure, people telling me I was selfish, or that they always felt like they had to walk on eggshells around me. So, the only thing I could think of was to remove myself from the equation, but for good. My counselor asked me, "Why didn't you go through with it?" I stated, "Because I would've proved them right." I felt that I would've been selfish to take my own life.

I know that suicide is real and so is the pain but I'm here to tell you that you don't have to go through that pain alone. You don't have to be your pain. You shouldn't have to. Jesus is waiting for you to let him in. He is knocking on the door to your heart that is intertwined with those emotions that are destroying you, and He wants you to let go of everything you're holding in.

Some people don't like counseling or the idea of opening up to a stranger. I get it, it's weird and uncomfortable. They probably don't even know what you're going through. You may not trust them with that information about your life, but it's someone with who you can communicate. If not, there's always Jesus. He is always listening even when you feel like He may not be. Honestly, I probably wouldn't be here if I didn't have a relationship with him.

To say that my suicidal thoughts just simply disappeared after a few counseling sessions would be a lie. I had several episodes, especially living on my own. There were too many rainy nights spent alone in my car thinking of how it would be if my life was just over. Too many rainy, cold, and lonely nights I've thought about just ending my life for good. Whenever these thoughts started to arise, I slowly learned to close my eyes and try to picture the good memories of my life, because even after all the terrible pain and loss I've experienced, I've had so many beautiful memories to be thankful for. So now, I simply close my eyes and remember the good in my life instead of the bad. I know, it's easier said than done, but I promise you with time if you train your mind to focus on the pure good, everything else will start to dwindle away, slowly, but surely.

I stopped going to counseling after a few sessions because personally, I thought Jesus was the best counselor for me. I committed to continue talking to Jesus not only when good things happen, but also through the hard times. It's the most precious way to spend my time and it's never wasted. He is with us during our lowest lows and our highest highs. He is with us on this Earth. Every time you see a rainbow after a rainy day, know that he is with us. Every wind that passes through your hair by the ocean breeze, know that he is with us. God isn't just in the heavens, but he is also with us on the ground.

Suffering

If I had to pick one book in the bible that has helped me most throughout my journey, it'd be the book of Job. This man lost everything. He lost his home, his sheep, camels, all his wealth, and his children. Yet, somehow, he still remained faithful to God. But even Job was human and experienced pain, so much so that he snapped. At the beginning of his suffering, he cursed his birthdate, not even wanting to be alive.

Just as I had thought of taking my own life, so did Job. He thought it would be better to not even had been born than to go through what he was going through. He was in pain physically, emotionally, and spiritually. *"At this, Job got up and tore his robe and shaved his head and said: Naked I came from my mother's womb and naked I will depart. The Lord gave and the Lord has taken away. May the name of the Lord be praised. In all this Job did not sin by charging God with wrongdoing."* (Job 1: 20-22 NIV). He expressed emotions as any other person would going through such tragic and excruciating loss. This example of Job shows that it is okay to go to God with any emotions you may be feeling. It is better to let them all out than to bottle them in.

When Job's friends first heard about his loss, *"Then they sat on the ground with him for seven days and nights. No one said a word to Job, for they saw that his suffering was too great for words"* (Job 2:13 NLT). After I had lost Aria, someone asked me what my advice was to say to someone who had just lost their child. Honestly, I thought I was in no way ready to answer that question because who am I to answer? But I was once that friend who lost a child. My response to them was simply, "Be present with them in their mourning. Tell them you hear them and you are here for them." Sometimes when we don't have the words to say, our presence is more than enough. *"Rejoice with those who rejoice; mourn with those who mourn."* (Romans 12:15 NIV). People will remember your presence, your warm hug of love, their tears becoming your tears. People will remember you being present with them more than your words.

During Job's journey of suffering, his friends began to mock him for his loss. They thought Job deserved this kind of suffering because he must've sinned. This is not always the case, though. Just because we sin doesn't mean that everything is going to get taken away. Satan was testing Job on his faith. No one but God knew what was happening in Job's life, not even Job himself! I think it's fair to say that we can never judge what someone is going through in life, especially when it comes to loss.

Job had many questions to ask God, as did I. For example, am I suffering because of all the sins I've committed? Am I not worthy? During my journey, I believed this lie, but that's all it was—a lie. When we go through suffering or pain, it is not always punishment. In Job's case, it was to mold and train him into becoming the faithful man that he is.

In the middle of the book, Job responds to his friends and confidently says, *"I know that my redeemer lives, and that in the end he will stand on earth."* *(Job 19:25 NIV).* Job had admirable faith that in the end, he was going to see God despite what he was going through, and Job didn't even know what he was going through.

Satan came to God thinking that Job wouldn't remain faithful if God took everything away, but in the end, God won and so did Job. Job was restored tenfold. God blessed him with fourteen thousand sheep and six thousand camels. God blessed him with not just one or two children, but ten! The ending of this book always gets me. The real question is, what if God never restored the blessings given to Job? The message or theme of this book though would not change because Job remained patient and faithful through his trials. Even if we are not restored to what we may have lost, there is still hope that we will gain so much more in eternity. If there is anything you can hold onto, let it be that one day your faith will be rewarded, if not on earth, then in heaven.

Comparison

Comparison isn't just a thief of joy or future hopes, it is a thief of living in the present moment. After I had lost Aria, even at my weakest state, comparison started to creep in. I compared myself to mothers before when I was pregnant with her, making sure I had the nicest maternity clothes, the coolest baby gadgets, and whatever else I needed to ensure I was prepared. I was a young mom, so I *needed* to look like I knew what I was doing. Physically I started comparing myself too. I had stretch marks everywhere and loose skin from my belly expanding. Other friends who I knew had kids didn't even have but one stretch mark! But now, I love my stretch marks. To this day I sometimes look a little longer at my stretch marks wishing they weren't there, but each mark is a memory and a reminder that my body is beautiful, and it is strong enough to hold life, a life that was my baby girl's and she got to live it with me.

My amazing prima bought me two books by other grieving mommas who had also experienced a hard loss: *Mending Tomorrow: Choosing Hope, Finding Wholeness by Alyssa* Quilala and *Heart Made Whole: Turning Your Unhealed Pain into Your Greatest Strength by Christa Black Gifford*. Reading about their loss, feeling every word that they wrote gave me peace in knowing that I was not alone in this pain. There is a community out there with other grieving mommas, and although I never imagined myself being part of this community, I know that God wants to use us all to share our hearts and our stories about our babies. I love that these two women found their hope or way of healing through Jesus. Even after reading these books though comparison whispered in my ear: *"But you're not as strong"*, *"You have no spouse like they do"*, *"Your faith is but little"*. I ate those lies up and they consumed me. You know what a lie is? It is a false statement, it is NOT true, and it is an imposture. You know what is not a lie? God's word and what he says about you: *"For you created my inmost being; you knit me together in my mother's womb. I praise you because I am fearfully and wonderfully made; your works are wonderful, I know that full and well."* (Psalms 139: 13-14 NIV). *"This is my command—be strong and courageous! Do not be afraid or discouraged. For the Lord your God is with you wherever you go."* (Joshua 1:9 NIV). *"And if God cares so wonderfully for flowers that are here today and thrown into the fire tomorrow, he will certainly care for you. Why do you have so little faith?"* (Luke 12:28 NLT). These verses are truths to lies that were whispered to me. So, when comparison or jealousy or whatever feeling may whisper in your ears, remind them of the truths that God says about you. My advice to you, grieving momma, or grieving dad, is that you can't compare your grief with someone else's grief. I know the world is still moving and going while yours seems like it is frozen in time, but remember you are not alone in it.

No pain, No gain

Pain is equivalent to discomfort. Sometimes when we are uncomfortable, we don't want to share it with anyone else. But you know who also experienced real-life pain? Jesus did. Romans 8:17-18 (NLT) states, *"And since we are his children, we are his heirs. In fact, together with Christ we are heirs of God's glory. But if we are to share his glory, we must also share his suffering. Yet what we suffer now is nothing compared to the glory he will reveal to us later."*

I can only speak from my personal experience but let me tell you that my whole perspective on pain has changed. My perspective on life and Jesus has changed. Life is hard and so is pain. But my God has miraculously helped me get through both. Every single day, he somehow managed to wake me up in the mornings when I did not want to wake. Every single day is a gift, and it's a gift from God that I will continue to cherish. God even brings gifts out of pain.

I'd like to believe that my ability to write this book is a gift, one that God placed on my heart to open up and to share not just my own personal experiences, but also my experience with him. Just because we live life for Christ doesn't mean that we will never come across pain or hardships. It's not a get-out-of-jail-free card. If we open our hearts and minds to this new perspective on pain, if we use it for good and not evil, beauty can come out of it. Just like working out, if you don't get through the hard sweats and tears, you will never see the outcome. It's a constant commitment and a day-by-day routine. All you need to do is take it one single step at a time and continue to look up and forward because the pain you experienced is behind you and you aren't going that way anymore.

The Strongest Momma

"Blessed is she who has believed that the Lord would fulfill his promises to her" (Luke 1:45 NIV).

What amazes me is that Jesus came down to this earth in the womb of a virgin. Let me repeat myself—Jesus came down to this earth as a baby, not a teenager or adult, but a baby. He went through the whole process of being in his mother's womb, being birthed into the world, and growing up around those he loved to help those he loved. Isn't that amazing?! And yes, if you aren't familiar with the story, Mary was a virgin, and she was also engaged to be married (betrothed) to a man named Joseph. I deeply admire Joseph for sticking by Mary's side through everything. They went through a lot as a couple as people began to start thinking Mary might have committed adultery. Joseph wanted to quietly divorce her until an angel visited him in a dream saying that *"Joseph, son of David, do not fear to take Mary as your wife, for that which is conceived in her is of the Holy Spirit"* (Matthew 1:20 ESV). What an honorable and faithful man to not only stay by Mary's side, but to also find humility in himself that he may not be worthy to be along this journey, but just like Mary he put his faith in God. This was a miracle and also a blessing for both of them.

In the book of Luke, the angel Gabriel came to Nazareth to greet Mary and to give her reassurance on this journey of becoming pregnant. *"She was thoroughly shaken, wondering what was behind a greeting like that. But the angel assured her, "Mary, you have nothing to fear. God has a surprise for you: You will become pregnant and give birth to a son and call his name Jesus."* (Luke 1:29-31 MSG). The bible is so real in how Mary reacted to the angel; *"Mary said to the angel, "But how? I've never slept with a man." The angel answered, "The Holy Spirit will come upon you, the power of the Highest hover over you; Therefore, the child you bring to birth will be called Holy, Son of God."* (Luke 1:34-35 MSG). Mary was a little uncertain, maybe even a little confused, but oh man, was she so faithful. *"I am the Lord's servant. May everything you have said about me come true.."* (Luke 1:38 NLT).

Mary was not only faithful in what the angel had told her, but she was faithful to the precious baby growing inside of her. When it came time to deliver the precious Child of God, Joseph and Mary had to travel to Bethlehem. It was a miraculous birth for everyone. The Inn they traveled to did not have any room, so they had to make other arrangements and stay in a cave-like place outside the Inn. It didn't matter to them where they were, what mattered was who they were going to be bringing into the world. No diaper bag ready, no plans set out, but they had each other, and they were ready.

Eight days after Jesus was born into the world, Mary and Joseph took him to Jerusalem to be dedicated. There they met a man named Simeon who was eager to meet this wonderful savior. The Holy Spirit was upon Simeon, and he was not going to die until he saw Jesus. As he finally gazed his eyes upon the Lord, he blessed them, and Mary and Joseph were in awe of what was being said about their precious baby. He was going to be a star! Has anyone ever spoken beautiful words over your beautiful baby? Although there were joyful words, there were also words of sorrow. Simeon said to Mary, *"Behold, this child is appointed for the fall and rising of many in Israel, and for a sign that is opposed (and a sword will pierce through your own soul also), so that thoughts from many hearts may be revealed."* (Luke 2:34-35 ESV).

Picture a sword going through your heart. That's painful. Now picture a sword going through your very own soul. This sword not only went through Mary's heart but her soul. It's hard to come back from something so excruciating. You can mend a broken heart, but a broken soul seems unfixable. A surgeon can fix a heart, but he can't fix a soul. Mary indeed witnessed both joyful and painful moments of being a mother. She watched him grow into a young man and the Child of God. Unfortunately, Mary had to also watch her son Jesus be beaten, bullied, and crucified. I cannot even begin to fathom what she was going through at that time. She wept and mourned like any other mother would for their child. Mary went through the worst kind of loss anyone on the face of this earth could ever go through.

No one knows that type of pain besides her and God. God knew she was going to come to this hard place of loss but did she? No way! Do you think if the angel told her what was going to happen to her child she would accept? Honestly, who knows. What I do know is that Mary was so strong, and she was so faithful.

Maybe at the time no one praised her for her strength, but clearly, God saw it in her from the beginning. God sees your strengths too, even if you don't. He sees so much more in us than we ever could in ourselves. The beautiful thing about this though is that if we want to see what he sees, where do we turn to? His word. Think of it as a mirror with affirming and loving words reflecting back at you, telling you that you are loved, you are strong, and you are seen. There's nothing but truth and good words that come from Jesus, and he's waiting for you to let him show you. In the end, Jesus rises from the dead and Mary gets to be reunited with not just her son, but her savior. Our savior. He is the only one who can graciously fix your broken heart and soul.

Part 6:

SURVIVING CHANGE

"God's loyal love couldn't have run out; his merciful love couldn't have dried up. They're created new every morning. How great your faithfulness! I'm sticking with God (I say it over and over). He's all I've got left." (Lamentations 3:22-24 MSG.)

I think this verse speaks for itself. His love and faithfulness do not cease. No matter what change we go through, he's all we have left. He never changes.

A New Beginning

One of the biggest changes of my existence here on earth was moving to another state by myself. I have always been a California girl, born and raised. Beautiful weather and sunshine all the time, but my days didn't feel like sunshine anymore. Change can be exciting, yet a fearful thing. But it was something I needed after all that had happened. I wanted a fresh start. I wanted to experience a new me, or better yet find the real me.

The opportunity to move to Washington State arose when I found out that my dad, stepmom, and sister had just moved back there after my father and gotten out of the military. I thought, why the heck not. A place where no one knows me, a place where I can start over. But of course, my mind began to have second thoughts. Will people think I'm running away from my problems instead of just facing them? But I had to remind myself I was going to do this for myself, even if I might be alone so that I can better myself and rediscover who I am.

During the almost nineteen-hour car ride with my father, my rollercoaster of emotions started to lead me to look back and think of how I could've been a better me for others back home, especially during my marriage. There was no more looking in the rearview mirror, but only to remember how far I've come and to appreciate where I am now and where I will be going.

Thankfully, I was able to transfer my job to Washington. I stayed with my family for a few months but realized I needed to be out on my own and experience the real world. I don't even know why I said I wanted to grow up fast and be an adult because if I could be a kid again, I would.

Being an adult on your own is hard, lonely, and scary. But it's also a season of growing, learning, and adjusting. Oh, and being broke. I can't forget about that part. When I found my first ever apartment I was in awe of the location. It was in this cute little town that had an amazing view of the ocean. I was sold and signed papers that day. Moving day came and although I was ready and excited, I wasn't really as ready as I thought I was going to be. I remember stressing out so much about bills, decor, furniture, tools, cleaning, cooking, etc. All of these things I had to learn on my own, with the exception of a phone call here and there to my family members (I am forever grateful for them).

With just a few bags, boxes, and a bed, I was moved in. Once my father left, I broke down in tears in the middle of my living room floor. I instantly started to pray over my apartment and for myself. I prayed for protection, that this new home would be a place for others to gather and of course to see what God was going to do with me here. I was not prepared for any of this. Are we ever really prepared for anything in life though? Even if we do prepare for something, the outcome may be different. For once in my life, I was okay with not knowing where I was going, just as long as I knew who was leading me there. I've realized now more than ever that even when the world around me changes, Jesus will forever be the only constant in my life. He is my anchor of hope even through the wildest waves of life.

Part 6: Surviving Change

Fast forward almost two years later, I'd say moving to Washington was one of the biggest, yet best, changes of my life. In my alone time here in this apartment, I got to write this book. I also got to experience the deep healing inside of me that I didn't know I still needed. Remember when people told me I should've screamed and cried at the top of my lungs once I found out Aria no longer had a heartbeat? Well, I did it all here in this apartment. God knew I was going to be here, that I needed to be here, and I am so thankful for that.

No matter where you go, where you move, or who you meet, there will always be problems. This time around, I knew who to give those problems to. I wasn't running away from my problems anymore, let alone handling them on my own. Now when problems arise in life I say, "Okay God, what shall *we* do?"

Community

Being around a community of people is a human trait that every person craves, and I was craving it as much as I craved eggnog on a chilly Christmas morning. I started to look on Google (thank God for the internet) for churches near me. I went "church hopping" to two different churches until I came across one that I truly fell in love with. I have to admit that going to a church where you know absolutely no one is quite eerie. The service was a bit different since there was worship after the sermon versus before. But I loved the environment and the community, so I went back again, again, and then again.

It was summertime and they had stands up for volunteers to help serve in the community. In my mind I thought, what better what to meet people than to help serve others? I met a beautiful couple who just had happened to be the pastors of the location I attended. I was delighted with the entire day. From that moment I created relationships with people who are now my dearest forever friends.

I was in awe. Here was little me from this small desert town now helping serve others who just might be new like me. The church ended up throwing a beautiful Thanksgiving dinner and I met one of the sweetest souls to ever walk the earth. She was one of the youth pastors and asked if I wanted to help out in youth culture. I was a little nervous so I told her I would think about it.

It only took me a day or two to think about it until I finally told her yes that I would do it. Then, COVID-19 happened.

Just as I was starting to get acquainted with a new community, I had to say goodbye. They decided to close the location I had attended, and I saw this is a sign that maybe it was time to move on. Then, God decided to step in. We turned this community into an online one. We began to reach out to people around the world! Little me had the honor to be a youth leader to not only kids here in the U.S., but all over the world. In the midst of people losing homes, jobs, and loved ones, I prayed that God would show me why I was still here, and he did. In the midst of the craziness going on in the world, I was still able to glorify him. He allowed me to share all this motherly love that was bottled up inside me and I finally got to share it with the youth.

God wants us to have community. Romans 15:5-7 ESV says, *"May the God of endurance and encouragement grant you to live in such harmony with one another, in accord with Christ Jesus, that together you may with one voice glorify the God and the Father of our Lord Jesus Christ. Therefore welcome one another as Christ has welcomed you, for the glory of God."* We were made to be in relationships with others. We were made to share the good news even when we felt like there was no good news to share at such a time as this. With God, there is always good news, because, in the end, he always wins.

I don't think anyone will forget about the year 2020. I'm sure there are going to be plenty of books written, and honestly, I hope so. I hope people take what the enemy made for evil and turn it into something good. Even if it isn't writing a book, maybe it's trying out a new hobby or having the courage to finally talk to that family member you haven't spoken to in years. Whatever it may be, I pray you find the courage to do it.

Community is so vital, and I am beyond blessed to have discovered such an amazing community as this. Find your community. Even if you are an introvert, I am sure you will find your fellow introverts introverting somewhere. Life can be lonely, but that doesn't mean we let that feeling tell us we have to be alone.

Science Only Goes So Far

I had a lot of complications with my body after giving birth. About a month after Aria was born, I had to go back to the hospital to get a D&C procedure.

Part 6: Surviving Change

My aunt told me that after I gave birth to Aria, I almost started bleeding out. The doctor's blue booties were covered in red. Nurses ran frantically in and out of the room. Sadly, I don't remember any of this. Maybe it was the drugs, maybe it was the numbness, or maybe God erased it from my memory because he knew I couldn't handle anything else. All I knew is that it was all unbearable.

My heaviness of bleeding reminded me of the story of the woman who bled for twelve years. During these times, no one wanted to be around someone who was looked upon as "dirty". She was unclean. *"A woman in the crowd had suffered for twelve years with constant bleeding, and she could find no cure. Comping up behind Jesus, she touched the fringe of his robe. Immediately, the bleeding stopped. "Who touched me?", Jesus asked. Everyone denied it, and Peter said, "Master, this whole crowd is pressing up against you." But Jesus said, "Someone deliberately touched me, for I felt healing power go out from me." When the woman realized that she could not stay hidden, she began to tremble and fell to her knees in front of him. The whole crowd heard her explain why she had touched him and that she had immediately been healed. "Daughter," he said to her, "your faith has made you well. Go in peace." (Luke 8:43-48 NLT).*

She was unclean but Jesus did not see her that way. Jesus saw her, and he saw her faith. Despite her many years of bleeding, she did not give up her faith in God. She remained active in her faith! Her faith in Jesus is what healed her. Our situation may not go away immediately as hers did, but oh boy does it give me hope to continue to remain active in my faith too!

My recovery to a fit and healthy body is still a process to this day. Before the pandemic happened, I went to doctors because I was experiencing excruciating cramping pains in my stomach. They ran several tests and did ultrasounds and I had to wait patiently for the results. I'd like to say I've become a patient person, but when it comes to my health or the health of any loved ones my patience becomes a little slim. A few days later, I got a call from the office stating that I had what is called adenomyosis. I didn't even know that was a thing let alone how to even spell or pronounce it. In a quick second, my mind immediately went into the negative zone. My hands started to shake as I tried typing in the diagnosis.

A Life After Loss

You know sometimes when we google things, we tend to automatically think things like, *oh no, am I going to die?* Or is that just me? I had discovered that I had tissue growing in the inside of my uterus, and the only way to get rid of the pain forever was to get rid of my uterus. Welp, there goes my luck with trying to have more kids in the future. Even if I did not get my uterus removed, any type of surgery or medical treatment would still not help increase my chances of getting pregnant in the future. Yes, Lord, I know I need a husband first, but would anyone even want to be with me if I could no longer have children? These were the lies I believed, and the enemy was winning.

I had visited my good friends for brunch a little after I had received the news and I did my best to put a smile on my face. She has an amazing husband and two beautiful daughters, one of which was the same age as Aria. I told her in a low tone of voice that my future was going to be one without any kids. My God-fearing, beautiful friend reminded me that God intends for us to be fruitful. In my mind I thought, well of course it's easy to say that when you have kids, but then she confidently reminds me that the word of God never fails and that his promises for us never fail.

It's sometimes hard for me to imagine myself having a child physically here with me on earth. I do sometimes let fear get the best of me, thinking about if I were ever to become pregnant again. What if I can't get pregnant again? Will I have to go through expensive medical treatments to conceive? Here come the lies from the enemy. When these lies arise, I have to remind myself, "*If my God doesn't view me as those lies, why should I?*"

I know barrenness is a sensitive topic for some, but like this book, I'm here to talk about the hard stuff. It's the things that pierce the heart or tongue of the ones who can't seem to find the words to share. It's hard to speak about things like this, but with God's guidance, I'm ready to speak about the unspeakable.

I like looking up words in the dictionary to discover the real meaning(s) of them. *Barren*; incapable of producing offspring; unproductive or unfruitful. There were several women in the bible who were barren: Sarah, Rebekah, and Rachel. The drama here in these stories between these women and their husbands is so real, it is one of the things I love about the Bible, it is so real.

Sarah was the wife of Abraham who was unable to bear him children (Genesis 16). She decided to take matters into her own hands and have Abraham sleep with her servant Hagar and she eventually gave him a son Ishmael. Hagar was Sarah's surrogate in this story. I can only imagine what Sarah was feeling: disappointment, frustration, sadness. Jacob was tricked into a marriage and ended up with two wives, Rachel and Leah, who were sisters! Jacob so deeply loved Rachel and worked hard to win her over from her father, but Leah was the first, and oldest, to lay with him and conceive a son; Rachel could not. When Rachel saw that she wasn't having any children for Jacob, she became jealous of her sister. She pleaded with Jacob, *"Give me children, or I'll die!" Then Jacob became furious with Rachel. "Am I God? He's the one who has kept you from having children!"* (Genesis 30:1-2 NLT). Rachel did the same act as Sarah did and had her husband sleep with her maid.

Rebekah's story was a little different. Although she too was unable to conceive, instead of taking matters into her own hands like the other women, her husband Isaac pleaded with the Lord (Genesis 25:21). Rebekah became pregnant with twins! Esau and Jacob were their names, and they were going to become two great and rival nations. By the grace of God, Sarah finally conceived a son at her old age and his name was Isaac. Yup, that's right! Isaac was the husband of Rebekah. It's wild to see the family tree picture here in these stories. After Rachel stopped trying to be in competition with her sister Leah, she decided to just pray to the Lord to have her own child, and he heard her prayer and honored it. *"Then God remembered Rachel's plight and answered her prayers by enabling her to have children. She became pregnant and gave birth to a son. "God has removed my disgrace," she said. And she named him Joseph, for she said, "May the Lord add yet another son to my family."* (Genesis 30:22-24 NLT). Wait, Joseph? As in Mary's husband Joseph? DANG. Some family tree, right?! Isn't it beautiful to see how much of an impact these children had on God's timing? It was HIS doing and HIS plan, not theirs.

To the mothers and fathers out there who have been trying to become pregnant, I cannot imagine all the trials and tribulations you've been through. My hope for you is that you persevere through this difficult season and continue to have faith that one day God will bless you with a beautiful child. He hears your prayers even when you think he is not listening.

You are more than barrenness. You are more than any diagnosis that a doctor may tell you. I know that no doctor, or diagnosis, is going to tell me who I am or who I will be! (cue *No Weapon by Fred Hammond*). Science only goes so far, and then comes our miraculous God. What a beautiful reminder that as children of God, we can truly overcome anything if we continue to have faith in him and his plans, not our own. We don't have to worry about our plans for the future because he already has them planned out for us. *"For I know the plans I have for you, declares the Lord, plans for welfare and not for evil, to give you a future and a hope."* (Jeremiah 29:11 ESV).

Memories

Social media can be great sometimes. One of the things I find fascinating about Facebook, for those who have one, is that they create memories of years past. Some memories may not be so great, while others are truly wonderful. There was one morning where I was struggling to find any form of strength to get through the day, and then I get a memory; July 5th, 2012, my sixteen-year-old self wrote a post that said, *"I am grateful for all of my problems. After each one was overcome, I became stronger and more able to meet those future problems that were still to come. I grew in all my difficulties, and I am happy with who I am today, stronger than ever."*

Maybe God was preparing me for such a time as this. God can take our messes and turn them into a message, or in this case, a post. No mess is too messy for God to clean up. We tend to focus on the messes or mistakes we have made in our lives rather than looking at how Jesus used those messes to bring you where you are now. Well, what if I don't like where I am now? My friend, there's only moving forward with Jesus. You don't ever have to worry or fret about going backward because he will always be certain to lead you to the right path, even when we may be torn between the two.

There might be a memory that replays in your head when a certain song comes on the radio, or when you are looking at old pictures. That memory may trigger sadness, or feelings of warmth and happiness. Either way, it's a day you once lived and, at that moment, you were completely present not having to fret about what tomorrow would bring. We may want to replay that memory, press rewind, or even delete it from existence, but at the end of the day, it will forever be ingrained in our hearts and our mind.

I wish I kept more memories of me being pregnant with Aria. I was so amazed at what my body could do with a little precious baby growing inside of me. I'd take pictures of my belly growing bigger, pictures of me in cute maternity clothes, or even record videos of her kicking me while lying on the couch. Now, I don't have those anymore, physically, because those memories reminded me of what I couldn't have, what I had lost. During my time of grieving, I discarded all the evidence of her ever really being with me. If I could go back in time and tell myself to not press delete, I'd do it in a heartbeat. Although I may no longer have pictures or recorded videos, I have stored it all in my heart.

What have you done in the act of grief or sadness? Is there a memory you'd like to replay in this present day? Well, you can. Take out that old photo album that's stored in the attic or your garage. If you're like me and have gotten rid of any existence of the memory you once longed to revisit, I hope you sit on that couch again and just close your eyes and remember. I hope you take that much-needed drive to that street you once said you'd never go on again. Or maybe it's going to that gravesite you haven't been to in years. Whatever it may be, I hope you treasure that moment and keep it safe in your heart.

Part 7

A HEART RENEWED

"My flesh and my heart may fail, but God is the strength of my heart and my portion forever." (Psalm 73:26 ESV).

Even through failures, we are reminded of where and who our strength comes from. My strength comes from within, and my heart is forever with God.

"You are so strong", is the phrase I would hear a lot. Would people still think that if they knew where my heart was at, where my thoughts were really at? I acted like I was strong whenever I went out in public, but behind closed doors, I was not. I did my best to try and put a smile on my face every single day because life goes on right? For others, it may have, but for me, it felt like my life had stopped. But life goes on, right? So, I guess I must too.

To this day I still get asked about Aria. Sometimes when I'm in group settings when people talk about their children or future children, I tend to stay silent until asked if I have my own, and honestly, sometimes I still say no. For some individuals, it's just a lot to take in all at once. For others, most don't even know what stillbirth is when I do explain it. This is another reason why I wanted to write this book, to speak about the things that our heart wants to say, even though it may be a little painful to do so. When you let your heart speak, I mean truly speak to others about what you've been through, it's like a new layer of your heart has opened up and it's strengthened from within.

Should you tell everyone about your loss? Well, that is entirely up to you to decide. For me, it depends on the setting and situation. I mean here I am telling you about it now via book, but not everyone is going to read this book. If it is heavy on your heart, let your heart speak about it. If you need assistance in what to say, pray.

Tin Man

Music really has a way to capture our every emotion. I remember putting together a playlist of emotional songs (don't act like you haven't done the same) and I came across one called *Tin Man* from Miranda Lambert. As she sang each word from that song, I couldn't help but cry and just think wow, this is how I feel. Has a song ever done that you? To sum up the song, she's basically telling the Tin Man that he can have her heart because it's no use to her anyway. No one else seems to want it either, so why should she keep it? This heart is not in perfect condition. It may even be smaller than your average. Hey, Mr. Tin Man, are you sure you want a heart that breaks and aches?

I put this different persona on for others when really, I just wanted to hide. Even with music, I knew I could just hide in my feelings. Hey, Mr. Tin Man, may I borrow your armor in exchange for my heart? I already felt so hollow inside so, what was there to lose? There might be a few scars on it, but it was still a heart. It was one that I never wanted back.

Here's the thing though; there's a difference between *being* strong and *acting* strong. When I had lost Aria, I couldn't distinguish between the two. Well, if I act like everything is okay, then I'm okay. If people see that I'm okay they can stop asking me if I'm really okay and I can stop lying by saying I'm okay when really, I am not. In all honesty, there were times people actually had stopped asking me when I needed them to ask me the most. I wanted them to ask me how I really was so I could just share how I was feeling with someone, anyone. I didn't want to keep it bottled up and explode again. It's crazy because even people who I thought were close to me never even asked me. Was it because they just didn't know how? Did they just want to leave me alone? I mean I didn't blame them, but didn't they want to know? Maybe the fake persona or armor was working.

Ephesians 6:10-11 (ESV) states, "Finally, be strong in the Lord and in the strength of his might. Put on the whole armor of God, that you may be able to stand against the schemes of the devil". Hey Mr. Tin Man, you can have your armor back. I think it's time for an upgrade. If this armor can help me stand against the evilest of evil, then this armor I shall wear and wear proudly. My friends, don't act strong with God, be strong with God! You are a child of God. You weren't meant to just wear a helmet or hold a sword, but to wear the whole armor of God. Stand tall in your armor and your faith knowing that nothing will come in between you and God.

Traditions

I absolutely love family traditions. There's just something so extravagant and special about them, especially when they get passed down from generation to generation. I wanted so badly to share that with Aria, but I could not. For her first birthday, family and friends gathered around her gravesite. We took photos and I thanked everyone for coming out. This day was hard for me. It was hard for everyone. It truly meant the world, seeing how much she was loved. How astonishing to see the love someone can give to others without even being here. We bought a beautiful rose-colored number one balloon for her and had beautiful flowers to go with it. Oh, and let me not forget the jeweled tiara to top it off because she was a princess, of course. I couldn't throw her a big birthday party, but I pictured her having one in heaven.

Year two came and it came in a blink of an eye. This year was especially hard because her father and I were no longer together. It was hard for me because I could not share with him my feelings of missing her and vice versa. I felt like I had failed her as a mother. But I knew I had so much more healing to do. That year, I decided to make my own tradition.

For the past four years, I went to her gravesite and put up a rose-colored number balloon. Some people may think it's weird to go visit her site since it's just her body there, but this was my family tradition with her. I don't know how long I will do it, but I will continue to do it for as long as I can.

On the day of her fourth birthday, I flew out to California, jumped off the plane, was picked up by my family and we went to the store and bought her a number four rose-colored balloon. While I was on the plane, I also decided to write her a note: *"Aria, I want to thank you for leading me closer to Jesus. There was a time when I didn't know what to believe anymore or even who to believe, but I was reminded of the precious love I received when you were with me, and I know that kind of love only comes from Jesus. And although you are not here, I still feel that love constantly in my heart. And if there is ever a day like today when it's just too much to handle, I'll just close my eyes and picture you with Jesus."*

So that's what I have done and will continue to do. I'll take a deep breath, close my eyes and picture her with Jesus. I have an angel in Heaven, and I get to call her my daughter. I don't know if you have any family traditions, but if not, it's never too late to make new ones. I will always celebrate the beautiful child that Jesus blessed me with. My hope for you is that you find some way to celebrate your loved one too.

A Spark in My Soul

You're probably wondering why I haven't shared how I was introduced to Jesus yet, but as they say, saved the best for last. I was a sophomore in high school when I got invited to a youth night by an old friend. My family talked about Jesus and I said my prayers at night, but I didn't know what a real relationship with him entailed. Looking back now, I can see clearly how he placed his hands over my family and I and protected us through all those years, and I didn't even know him yet. How incredible is that?!

That evening at group we talked about going to a concert in Las Vegas called "Winter Jam". A free trip and music? Count me in! Little did I know that on the journey to Las Vegas, I was going to a place of worship and would meet some of the most beautiful people who would speak and sing more about Jesus. I saw Dara Maclean, For King and Country, Newsboys and so many more talented artists. That evening I experienced a spark inside me, a warm feeling that I had never felt before and it was a feeling that I never wanted to go away. It's hard to explain, but have you just ever felt that overwhelming sensation inside of you that gives you chills all around your body, makes your heart grow a size or two bigger, and makes your eyes fill with tears of joy? You may have felt that spark inside of you a little differently than I may have that evening, but that my friend, that is the feeling of the Holy Spirit. That spark is the feeling of Jesus coming into your soul and saying welcome home.

Unfortunately, after I graduated high school that feeling went away. Out into the real world I would go, thinking I could handle everything on my own. Silly eighteen-year-old me was not as ready as she thought she would be. Have you ever been introduced to someone, maybe start a conversation with them and say hello nice to meet you, but never really get to know them? Have you ever needed someone to help you and then afterward just forget they were ever there? That was what my relationship with Jesus looked like. Only when it was convenient for me would I ask for his help and then go on about my day.

There was one person in the bible who also was introduced to God and then went about their everyday life, except this person was a King and had other duties to attend to. King David wrote in Psalm 42:5 (ESV), *"Why are you cast down, O my soul, and why are you turmoil within me? Hope in God; for I shall again praise him, my salvation and my God."* The keyword here for me is *again. I shall again praise him.* If you have been introduced to Jesus and feel like it's too late for you to start a relationship with him after all you have done, let me tell you that it is never too late. Jesus is already waiting for you to let him back into your life (or in your life for the first time) and wants to celebrate every day and every minute with you. After losing Aria and my marriage, I couldn't bear the thought of how the look on God's face would be. Would he be disappointed with my divorce or my lack of faith? At this point of my life, I needed to feel that spark again inside me, that warmth inside my soul that says, "I am home." I am home again with God and until the day I die, I will continue to praise him. Are you ready to come home?

Part 8:

A LIFE AFTER LOSS

"I'm not saying that I have this all together, that I have it made. But I am well on my way, reaching out for Christ, who has so wondrously reached out for me. Friends, don't get me wrong. By no means do I count myself an expert in all of this, but I've got my eye on the goal, where God is beckoning us onward—to Jesus. I'm off and running, and I'm not turning back." (Philippians 3:12-14 MSG).

I'm no expert at life or loss, but I know where I want to go. I want to run to Jesus, and I don't intend on looking back.

as anyone ever asked you that cliché question, "Where do you see yourself in 5 years?" I remember getting asked that question so many times when I was a senior in high school. In my mind, I *thought traveling the world, duh*, but my real response was *I don't know*. Some of my friends had their lives planned out, but I did not. Many times, we can try to paint a picture of what our future is going to look like, but in reality, it never looks like how we pictured it. We can pick the size of the canvas we want, what brushes to use to define certain moments in time, use an eraser to forget about the bad ones, but whatever picture we end up creating, God somehow always finds a way to make it better.

At the moment the picture may not look clear, but watching God take control of the paintbrush instead of you creates the clearest and most beautiful picture we can ever fathom. I know I wouldn't erase a thing.

There is a life after loss, friends. Psalms 30: 11-12 (NLT) says, *"You have turned my mourning into joyful dancing. You have taken away my clothes of mourning and clothed me with joy, that I might sing praises to you and not be silent. O Lord my God, I will give you thanks forever!"*. He turns mourning into dancing. The dancing may not come naturally at first, but when you step into the Lord's presence of joy, you won't care who you are dancing in front of. It may seem more like arms waving in the air before it looks like the cupid shuffle, but whatever dancing may be like for you, I pray you will find true joy in the midst of it and embrace it fully, even if you can't dance, do it anyway!

I know this world holds so much evil and darkness, but there is still so much beauty to be seen. And some of that beauty comes from within you.

You know the song that goes, *"This little light of mine, I'm gonna let it shine?"* Well, that's exactly what you need to do. Let it shine! No matter how little you think your light may be, it could be bigger for someone else. *"In the same way, let your light shine before others, that they may see your good deeds and glorify your Father in heaven."* (Matthew 5:16 NIV).

So, if my twenty-five-year-old self, almost to thirty self, gets asked the question again of where I see myself in five years, my response would still most likely be, *I don't know.* This time around though, I do know who I am trusting with my life. Every day and every step of the way I am trusting in Jesus because his picture of my life is far more captivating than mine could ever be. Just like a beautiful cotton candy sunset filling the skies, I am reminded of how astonishing God's canvas is.

Whenever God is finished with my picture, when my time on earth has come to an end, I know I can look at that picture and say, *"Thank you, God, it was truly beautiful."* You still have time to create infinite beautiful memories that will eventually transcend into one big picture that is your life. I hope that it is colorful, filled with love and laughs, but most importantly filled with love and lots of it. Your life after loss has just begun.

Part 8: A Life After Loss

Aria's Obituary:

September 1, 2016, Aria Monet Guinn was born weighing 6 lbs. 13 oz. and was 19 ¼ in. long. Aria was born to her parents but was received in eternity by our Father God. She is a beloved daughter, granddaughter, great-granddaughter, cousin, and niece. We believe that Aria has touched many, many hearts and will continue to do so. She is our greatest and most precious gift from God and for that, we are grateful we had the chance to experience 9 beautiful months with her while she was in her mother's womb. Although this is a difficult time for us, we find comfort in the fact that if we continue to live for Jesus, we will see her again. Aria has blessed us with a love that we have never experienced before. Thank you, God, for our baby girl.

March of Dimes Speech:

This speech was difficult to write, much like this book, but it brought so much healing to me and I am so happy God gave me the opportunity to share it with others. I pray that you too find the strength and courage to share your story with others.

"I know so many of you here today have a story just like ours. All of us here today are connected either by a shared experience or a shared commitment to helping families experience the joy of a healthy baby. I would like to take this moment and share with you all one of my new favorite quotes from the hit TV show This Is Us. "You took the sourest lemon that life has to offer and turned it into something resembling lemonade." I'd like to think of this opportunity to be in front of you all today and sharing our daughter's story as a chance to turn something so bitter into something so sweet. September 1st will forever be a day of celebrating a life that was taken too soon. That morning the most piercing words came from the doctors' mouth "I'm sorry but there is no heartbeat". That loud and strong heartbeat of hers that we had heard just days before was no longer there. After about 16 hours of labor, I gave birth to a beautiful baby girl named

A Life After Loss

Aria. Although her wings were ready, our hearts were not. You see, stillbirth is not an easy thing to talk about, but today I am here to break that silence because no parent should have to ever endure that feeling of leaving a hospital empty-handed and no parent should have to ever wonder why. March of Dimes continues to work hard to ensure that no family has to ever go through that kind of pain. Every child has a purpose in this world. So, if they are here with you today, hold on extra tight to their precious little hands, and if they are not, continue to hold on to them close to your heart until you can hold them in your arms again. Today with every step we take we celebrate the ones who have fought and conquered through their battles, but we also remember and celebrate the ones who did not. Thanks to the March of Dimes, we are one step closer to ensuring that all babies get to go home happily with their families. So today let's march towards a better tomorrow." (April 21, 2018).

ACKNOWLEDGMENTS

o my mother and stepfather, a.k.a gigi and papa, I don't know where I would be without the both of you. Thank you for allowing me to vent to you both during this process. What was once a crazy idea is now a reality and I can't thank you both enough. I love ya'll tons.

To my father and stepmother, thank you so much for being there for me during such a hard season. I love you both more than your hearts or minds could ever imagine.

To my siblings, thank you for reminding me why I love being a big sister so much. Ya'll make life worth living for, even when it gets crazy! I sibling swear to cherish each moment that we spend together. Yaya loves you.

To Tawny, what was once a journal filled with endless words of a story my heart was trying to tell, you helped me turn it into this book. I am eternally grateful for you and our friendship!

To my family and friends in California, thank you all so much for being my biggest cheerleaders. La familia forever.

To my Pacific Northwest family and friends, thank you for opening your arms to me in a time where I felt alone. It was in this season I wrote my book and was welcomed into a community that I know will last a lifetime.

CPSIA information can be obtained
at www.ICGtesting.com
Printed in the USA
BVHW041346280921
617682BV00019B/597